Photo by Martha Swope Associates (Carol Rosegg)

Molly Ringwald, Julie Heberlein and Don Bloomfield in a scene from the New York production of "Lily Dale." Set by Daniel Conway; costumes by Deborah Shaw.

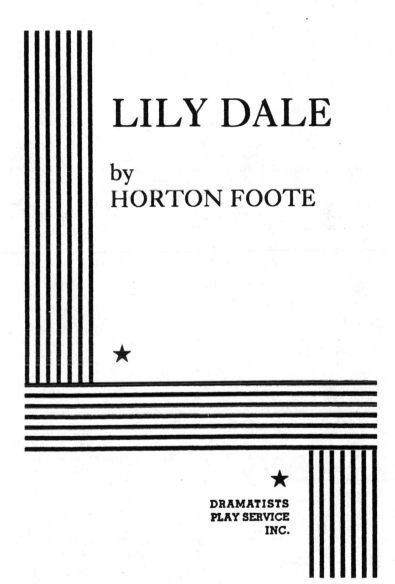

LILY DALE

by
HORTON FOOTE

DRAMATISTS
PLAY SERVICE
INC.

LILY DALE
Copyright © 1987, Horton Foote
Copyright © 1979, Horton Foote
as an unpublished dramatic composition

All Rights Reserved

LILY DALE had its world premiere on November 20, 1986 at the Samuel Beckett Theatre, New York City. It was directed by William Alderson with sets by Dan Conway, lights by John Hastings, costumes by Deborah Shaw and wig and hair design by Paul Huntley. The Production Stage Manager was Laura Kravets. The cast, in order of appearance, was as follows:

HORACE ROBEDAUX.................. Don Bloomfield
MRS. COONS............................. Jane Welch
LILY DALE ROBEDAUX................ Molly Ringwald
CORELLA DAVENPORT................ Julie Heberlein
PETE DAVENPORT....................... Greg Zittel
WILL KIDDER........................... Johnny Kline
ALBERT THORNTON .... Cullen Johnson

The play takes place over a period of three weeks. On a train to Houston, Texas, in the home of Pete Davenport, in Houston, and on the train back to Harrison, Texas. The time is late Fall, 1909.

ACT I

Scene 1 Morning
Scene 2 Later that afternoon
Scene 3 A few hours later
Scene 4 Two hours later

ACT II

Scene 1 Two weeks later
Scene 2 A few days later
Scene 3 Later that night
Scene 4 One week later
Scene 5 The next day

CHARACTER DESCRIPTIONS

HORACE ROBEDAUX: *19 years old, emotional, optimistic and a survivor.*

MRS. COONS: *Late 40's to 50's, lively, opinionated and displays a religious Baptist fervor.*

LILY DALE ROBEDAUX: *18 years old, emotional, strong willed, self involved. A feminine, southern belle. Plays the piano with enormous confidence and little talent.*

CORELLA DAVENPORT: *38 years old. Widowed but remarried mother of Horace and Lily Dale. Wife to Pete Davenport. Strong character, motherly, compassionate and a survivor. Also a work horse.*

PETE DAVENPORT: *Late 30's early 40's. Stepfather to Horace and Lily Dale. Corella's husband. Hard working, inflexible, opinionated with conservative values.*

WILL KIDDER: *22 years old. Likeable, enthusiastic, confident. Lily Dale's beau.*

ALBERT THORNTON: *Early 40's. Corella's older brother. Easy going, cheerful.*

SET DESCRIPTION

The action of the play takes place in the living room of Pete Davenport's two story home in turn of the century Houston, Texas, 1909. The living room is small and simply furnished. The main entrance to the set is Upstage Left via the front door which opens on to a small entrance hallway. This leads to the living room. The entrance hallway leads Off Right to Pete and Corella Davenport's bedroom, Lily Dale's bedroom, and the kitchen. An additional, smaller doorway leads from the living room Upstage Right to the entrance hallway.

The room is decorated with tongue-in-groove wainscot and above the chair rail is a light-colored turn of the century wallpaper which has faded slightly with time.

The room is simply furnished with the exception of Lily Dale's brand new upright piano located against the Stage Right wall. Downstage of the piano is a young lady's slipper chair of the period. Upstage of the piano is a crank Victrola on a small table. A large, worn Oriental rug is centered on the living room floor. Upstage to the right of Center is a furniture grouping consisting of a large Morris chair, a foot stool and a table with a glass shade lamp. This area is used primarily by Mr. Davenport.

Directly Upstage Center against the wall to the right of the main entrance is a small, single chair, without arms, which is used as an extra chair and is moved about the room. Along the Stage Left wall is an additional lamp on a low end table and a period sofa. Directly behind the sofa are two large windows covered with simple lace curtains. Downstage of the couch is a small wooden trunk that Lily Dale uses to hide her valuables.

In the Downstage Left corner of the room stands a cast iron parlor stove. The Downstage Left section of the wall that contains the stove pivots Upstage opening the wall to reveal a double train seat above which is a luggage rack. The opening and closing scenes are played here.

LILY DALE

ACT I
Scene 1

As the lights are brought up Down Left, we see Horace Robedaux, 19, seated and looking out of the train window. A woman in her late forties comes in. She is Mrs. Coons. The movement of the train can be heard underneath the scene.

MRS. COONS. Mind if I sit beside you, son?

HORACE. No, Ma'am.

MRS. COONS. I can't stand a train trip without a little company. I wouldn't care to ask to sit beside those older gentlemen. They might think I was forward. They're all drummers you know I can tell by looking at them. *(She looks at Horace.)* How old are you, young man?

HORACE. Nineteen.

MRS. COONS. When's your birthday?

HORACE. In April.

MRS. COONS. In April! I have a boy just your age. He'll be twenty in June. Almost your age that is. Two months younger. Where are you going?

HORACE. Houston.

MRS. COONS. Another coincidence, so am I. Houston your home?

HORACE. No, Ma'am. I'm going on a visit.

MRS. COONS. Who are you visiting? Your grandma?

HORACE. No, my mother.

MRS. COONS. Your mother? Not your mother and your daddy?

HORACE. No, Ma'am, my daddy is dead; she's married again.

7

MRS. COONS. Did you used to live with them in Houston?

HORACE. No, Ma'am. My stepfather doesn't have a whole lot and it's all he can do to take care of my sister and mother.

MRS. COONS. Oh, well, times are hard all over. I think they'll get better, though, don't you?

HORACE. I certainly hope so.

MRS. COONS. So do we all. I have a rich uncle, thank God ... from New Orleans. When things get too tight, I just write dear Uncle Julius, and I say, "Here I am begging again." He's real sweet about it, too, just sends me whatever I need. Hardest part for me is my mama. Now I've known nothing but lean times all my life, so naturally, I don't know anything different. But Mama, she was born with a golden spoon in her mouth to hear her tell it. And being poor has been a real cross to her. You got on the train in Harrison. Do you live there?

HORACE. No, Ma'am. I used to. I live in Glen Flora now. I've been working there at the general store.

MRS. COONS. Well, I live in Harrison now. Been there two months ... like it real well. I used to live in Houston, but my husband lost his job there and got a position at the gin in Harrison. He's a bookkeeper. I hope he'll keep that. *(A pause.)* We have a problem. My husband that is. He drinks. He does fine on a job and then he gets to drinking after two or three months and they let him go. He's taken the Keeley Cure more times than I can count but so far nothing seems to help. He swears this time he's learned his lesson. I hope to goodness he has. I'm going in now to see about shipping our furniture out to Harrison. We just sold our home in Houston. We won't buy a house in Harrison until we see if we are going to be permanent.

HORACE. Whose house are you renting in Harrison?

MRS. COONS. They call it the old Robedaux place. They say it's a sad house. The man was a brilliant lawyer and drank himself right into the grave. Mr. Coons said...

HORACE. That was my house. At least it was my father's. I lived there until I was eight. Until my mama and daddy separated.

MRS. COONS. Separated? Oh, mercy! What a terrible thing. I

hope it didn't end in divorce?

HORACE. No, Ma'am.

MRS. COONS. Did your mama and daddy reconcile before he died?

HORACE. No, Ma'am.

MRS. COONS. Have you been inside that house lately?

HORACE. No, Ma'am.

MRS. COONS. Well, it is awful rundown. We're paying twelve dollars a month rent but I swear it's not worth it. It leaks like a sieve. I don't know when it's been painted. The yard is full of weeds. *(A pause.)* Is it your daddy died a drunkard?

HORACE. Yes, Ma'am.

MRS. COONS. I feel sorry for you, son. Deeply sorry. I know what that can mean. I get on my knees every night praying Mr. Coons will lose his taste for it. I hope your stepdaddy don't drink.

HORACE. No, Ma'am. Not that I know of.

MRS. COONS. Thank God for that. Pansy Greenwood is my best friend. She's been married three times now. Everyone has turned out to be a drunkard except for the last and he's a morphine addict. That's the worst of all. I tell Billie Joe ... that's my boy. Thank God, Daddy ain't a morphine addict. *(A pause. She sighs dolefully and then looks up at Horace.)* Are you a Christian, son?

HORACE. Yes'm. I guess so.

MRS. COONS. What do you mean you guess so, son? There's no guessing about being a Christian. You're either saved or not. Are you baptized?

HORACE. I don't know, Ma'am.

MRS. COONS. You don't know?

HORACE. No'm.

MRS. COONS. Why don't you know?

HORACE. Well, I hadn't thought about it one way or the other. If I was baptized, I was too young to remember it.

MRS. COONS. Mercy! You ask your mama the first thing you see her. You ask her if you're baptized. Your soul is in terrible danger, if you're not, son. An' don't you put that question off. That's all Satan

9

would have you do is postpone that question. Do you attend church?

HORACE. No, Ma'am.

MRS. COONS. You don't?

HORACE. No, Ma'am. The church my people go to doesn't have a congregation in Glen Flora.

MRS. COONS. What church is that?

HORACE. The Episcopal.

MRS. COONS. I guess they don't. They only have a small one in Harrison. *(Proudly.)* I'm a Baptist.

HORACE. Yes, Ma'am.

MRS. COONS. My mama was a Baptist and her mama before her. We have churches everyplace. Black and white. We're flourishing. If we'd baptized you, you would have known it.

HORACE. Yes, Ma'am.

MRS. COONS. I was baptized in the river. Made clean in the river. Gave all my sins to Jesus in the river. Washed in the blood of the lamb in the river. I'm ready to meet my Maker, son. I am ready. I am ready. *(A pause.)* Did you go to school in Harrison?

HORACE. As far as the sixth grade ... then I quit.

MRS. COONS. Billy Joe wants to quit but I beg him not to. Didn't your mama try to get you to stay in school?

HORACE. No, Ma'am. She didn't have any education to speak of. She only went to the fourth grade. And my stepfather only got as far as the second grade. *(A pause.)* My father was an educated man ... all his family were. They were Greek scholars and Latin scholars. You know the *Harrison Spectator*?

MRS. COONS. Read it every week.

HORACE. My uncles started that. One of them never worked at all, they say. He just sat around and read books in Greek all the time. My mother says she'd rather see me dead than that way. She said he lived a useless life. *(A pause.)* I like to read though. I can't help it. I don't tell my mother because it would worry her. But I read all the time ... newspapers and magazines and books about famous men. I don't care for novels.

MRS. COONS. And the Bible, son. Do you read your Bible?

10

HORACE. No, Ma'am.

MRS. COONS. Oh, poor child. Why not?

HORACE. I don't have a Bible.

MRS. COONS. You don't have a Bible?

HORACE. No, Ma'am.

MRS. COONS. Son, what are you going to say to your Maker when he asks you that question, "Did you read your Bible?" An' you say, "No, Sir." And he says, "Why not?" An' you say, "Because I had no Bible." An' he says, "Why not?" What will you say?

HORACE. I don't know.

MRS. COONS. You better think up a good answer, son. Because that question is coming to you one of these days. An' my heart trembles for you when I think of the wrath of my God. Get yourself a Bible, son. Promise me that. Promise me you'll get yourself a Bible and ask your mama about your baptism, and if you're not baptized, see that you have it done right away. Do you say your prayers every night?

HORACE. No, Ma'am.

MRS. COONS. Then you start praying every day. On your knees ... morning and night. You can hear me praying all over town. Mr. Coons says, "Mrs. Coons you're praying too loud, you're keeping people awake with your prayers." "It's good for them," I say ... "Let them hear the prayers of a true Christian." An' I just pray that much louder. Why sometimes I even shout. Shouting down the devil, I say. An' you have to shout loud to shout down the devil. Would you join me in a little prayer now, son?

HORACE. No, Ma'am. That's all right. I don't believe so.

MRS. COONS. Don't be embarrassed, son. Never be ashamed to let people know you're a Christian. *(She prays.)* Father, take this boy here... *(She turns to Horace.)* What's your name, son?

HORACE. Horace.

MRS. COONS. Horace. Cleanse Horace of his worldly ways, Father. Open his eyes to the need of Baptism. *(She continues praying as the lights fade. The sound of the train gets louder for a moment. Then slowly fades out.)*

11

SCENE 2

As the lights are brought up, we hear Lily Dale, 18, Horace's sister, small boned, thin and delicate, practicing at an upright piano. She is playing the Mozart Sonata in C Major. There is a knock at the door. She doesn't hear it at first and continues playing. There is another knock. She hears this, stops playing and calls...

LILY DALE. Mama ... Mama...

CORELLA. *(Her mother, 38, enters U.R.)* What is it, Lily Dale?

LILY DALE. Someone is at the door, Mama.

CORELLA. Can't you open the door, honey?

LILY DALE. I'm scared to, Mama.

CORELLA. Lily Dale, heavens!

LILY DALE. Doris Violet tells me the city is alive with beggars and gypsies and White Slavers. She says her mother forbid her ever to open her door.

CORELLA. I think that's a good idea when you're alone, honey, but I don't think you have to worry when I'm in the house. *(Again a knock.)* Just a minute. *(She opens the door. Horace is there.)* Horace... *(She embraces him.)* Lily Dale, it's Horace.

LILY DALE. *(Going over to him.)* Hello, Brother. *(She hugs him.)* We thought you were the gypsies. Mr. Davenport is in Atlanta seeing his kin, and Mama and I are here alone in the city. And my girlfriend, Doris Violet, says it is dangerous for ladies and young girls to be alone in this wicked city, as it is filled with gypsies and beggars and White Slavers. You heard about Charlie Parker?

HORACE. No, I don't believe I did.

LILY DALE. Well ... he didn't live in Houston but in Philadelphia ... and one day he went out to play and the gypsies came by and grabbed him and took him off, and he has never been seen or heard of by his family until this very day ... An' Mama was on the porch last week and this beggar man came by all bandaged up and he stopped and asked her if she would fix his bandages as they were coming loose. So she invited him up on the porch and she began to retie them for him and he reached out an' tried to grab her.

CORELLA. Yes, he did, Son. Like to have scared me to death ... I screamed and ran into the house as fast as I could and locked every door in the house.

LILY DALE. The city is filled with danger, Brother. The White Slavers put a pill in your tea or coffee that knocks you out and then they carry you off to China and force you to become a prostitute.

HORACE. Is that right?

CORELLA. Yes, a girl has to be very careful in the city, Son.

HORACE. Yes, Ma'am. I guess so.

CORELLA. Did you take the streetcar here from the station?

HORACE. Yes, Ma'am.

LILY DALE. How do you like my piano?

HORACE. That's nice, Lily Dale.

LILY DALE. When Mama and Mr. Davenport first got married, he said he had always wanted a daughter and though he weren't a rich man, he was going to spoil me in all ways and make up for the daddy I never had. And my heaven, he has. He got me a second-hand piano straight off and then after I learned to play some, he said he wouldn't have me using a secondhand piano and went out and bought this one for me.

HORACE. Well, that is sure a nice piano.

LILY DALE. Oh, he's so sweet to me, Brother. He is the best thing that ever lived. My own daddy, if he had lived, couldn't have been sweeter to me ... could he, Mama?

CORELLA. No, precious.

LILY DALE. He bought this dress for me from Munn's just before he left for Georgia and, Brother, he has to work so hard.

HORACE. Is that so?

LILY DALE. Oh, yes. He is up at four every morning and then he takes the streetcar to the railroad yards and he works there until four in the afternoon and he comes home and then he works out

13

back until way dark in his garden.

HORACE. My goodness.

LILY DALE. And then he comes in and he's so tired he can't eat and he sits here, and while Mama is getting his supper, I take off his shoes and get him a pillow to rest his head on and then I go to the piano and I play him an Etude of Chopin.

HORACE. Do you?

LILY DALE. Yes. Chopin is his favorite, he says. Brother, you haven't heard me play the piano, have you?

HORACE. No.

LILY DALE. Want me to play for you now?

CORELLA. Honey, your brother just got here. He's tired. Let him rest for a while first. What time were you up this morning?

HORACE. Four. Randall, the colored man that works with me in the store, brought me into Harrison in Mr. Galbraith's wagon. I caught the seven o'clock train.

CORELLA. Did you have breakfast?

HORACE. Yes, Ma'am. Randall's wife fixed me a big breakfast.

LILY DALE. We know all about getting up early in the morning. Mr. Davenport is up every morning at four. Even on Sundays. Isn't he, Mama?

CORELLA. Yes, he is. Horace, you've grown. Stand up. Let me take a good look at you. *(He does so.)* You've turned into a fine-looking young man.

HORACE. Thank you.

CORELLA. Do you realize it's a year since we've seen each other?

LILY DALE. How long are you planning to stay, Brother?

HORACE. Oh, I don't know exactly, you mentioned a week in your letter and...

CORELLA. *(Interrupting nervously.)* Are you hungry, Son?

HORACE. Well...

CORELLA. If I fixed a sandwich, could you eat it?

HORACE. Sure.

CORELLA. And I have a cake I made this morning. Would you

like a piece of that, too?

HORACE. Yes, Ma'am. *(Corella exits U.R. Horace looks around.)* Is this a two-story house?

LILY DALE. Yes, it is. We rent the upstairs to a quiet couple that work all day. They get up at four, too. They are in bed by eight. Do you think I've changed?

HORACE. Yes, you have.

LILY DALE. Would you have recognized me if you'd passed me on the street?

HORACE. I think so.

LILY DALE. I keep having this terrible dream that I'm kidnapped and they won't let me go until I'm an old woman, and I come back home and no one recognizes me ... An' I keep saying, "I'm Lily Dale. Lily Dale Robedaux." But no one will believe me. Did you ever have a dream like that?

HORACE. No.

LILY DALE. Do you ever have dreams?

HORACE. Sometimes.

LILY DALE. What about?

HORACE. Oh, I don't know. Once I dreamed ... *(Pause.)* I forget.

LILY DALE. We didn't think you were coming when you didn't answer Mother's letter.

HORACE. I didn't get the letter right away and when I did get it, I just decided to come on.

LILY DALE. How much did it cost you to get here?

HORACE. Two dollars.

LILY DALE. Where did you get two dollars?

HORACE. Mama sent it to me.

LILY DALE. She did? Did you ask her for it?

HORACE. No, she just sent it to me.

LILY DALE. How are you gonna get back?

HORACE. Mama said she would give me two dollars to get back after I got here.

LILY DALE. You have a job, don't you?

HORACE. Yes.

15

LILY DALE. How much do you get paid a week?

HORACE. Three dollars.

LILY DALE. Some of my friends have jobs, but Mr. Davenport said he won't hear of me working.

HORACE. Is that right?

LILY DALE. He spoils me in every way. See my shoes? He bought them just before he left.

HORACE. They're very pretty, Lily Dale.

LILY DALE. They were very expensive. I miss him. I'll be glad when he comes home.

HORACE. How much longer will he be gone?

LILY DALE. He was to be gone three weeks, but we got a letter yesterday and he said things had changed so in Atlanta, it didn't seem like home any longer and he longed to get back to us. So he's cutting his trip short.

HORACE. Oh, I see.

LILY DALE. He didn't say how much though. When Mama got the letter, she said it was a blessing you hadn't come, because she would be a nervous wreck having you here and expecting Mr. Davenport to walk in any minute, unexpected. You see, she sent for you behind his back.

HORACE. Did she?

LILY DALE. She kind of hinted around for his permission to ask you here while he was gone, but he said he didn't think it would be a good idea to encourage you to take off from work, and so she didn't press it any further.

HORACE. Oh.

LILY DALE. But then she decided to write you anyway ... which I thought at the time was a mistake. I always think deceit is a mistake. Don't you? *(Corella enters U.R. with a glass of milk and a sandwich. She hands them to Horace.)* I told Brother about Mr. Davenport coming home. Why didn't you tell me you sent him two dollars for a ticket?

CORELLA. It was my own secret, honey. I have to have a few secrets.

LILY DALE. Does Mr. Davenport know you gave him that

16

money?

CORELLA. No, and I don't want you to tell him. You hear me?

LILY DALE. Can I play the Etude for you now, Brother?

HORACE. Sure.

LILY DALE. Mr. Davenport says he'd take his last cent to pay for my music lessons. Do you have musical ability, Brother?

HORACE. I don't know. *(Lily Dale goes to the piano. She does not play well, but with enormous confidence. She plays the Chopin Etude in C Minor.)* Mama, I was hoping that I...

CORELLA. *(Again nervously interrupting him.)* Have you been to Harrison lately? *(She crosses R. to get the laundry basket, brings it back to the couch and begins to fold the clothes.)*

HORACE. I try to get in every week. I get up early Sunday morning and I walk into Harrison along the railroad tracks, and have Sunday dinner with Aunt Virgie or Aunt Inez or sometimes Aunt Gladys. Then I get up early Monday morning and walk back to Glen Flora in time to get the store open.

CORELLA. How long does it take you to walk it?

HORACE. Three hours. Aunt Virgie has taught me to dance.

CORELLA. She would. You can't be around Virgie for five minutes without some kind of dancing going on.

LILY DALE. *(Stops playing and turns to them.)* I'm not going to play any more if you all are going to talk.

CORELLA. I'm sorry, Sister. *(Lily Dale begins again. Horace listens for a moment.)*

HORACE. *(Speaking while Lily Dale is playing.)* Mama... *(Lily Dale stops.)*

CORELLA. Shh ... Shh *(Whispering.)* We'll talk when Lily Dale finishes. She's very sensitive. *(Again there is a silence as Lily Dale continues to play. Horace, after a few moments, begins to nod and then falls fast asleep. Soon he begins to snore. Lily Dale hears this and stops playing.)*

LILY DALE. Mama ... he's asleep. I think that's very rude of him.

CORELLA. *(Crosses to Lily Dale.)* He doesn't mean to be rude,

Lily Dale. I just don't think he's used to hearing music like that and he's probably very tired from the train ride.

LILY DALE. How long is he planning to stay?

CORELLA. I don't know. When I invited him, I asked him to stay a week, but that was before I knew about Mr. Davenport cutting his trip short. I'm going to tell him he can't stay more than a day.

LILY DALE. What would you do if Mr. Davenport walked in right now?

CORELLA. I'd die, Lily Dale.

LILY DALE. What do you think Mr. Davenport would say?

CORELLA. I don't know. I just pray he doesn't come until Horace leaves. *(Pause.)* I don't think Mr. Davenport will come home before the day after tomorrow. We got his letter yesterday and it takes two days from Atlanta. *(Horace wakes up.)* You've been asleep. You had a good nap.

HORACE. Oh, I didn't know where I was for a minute.

LILY DALE. How long do you plan on staying, Brother?

HORACE. I had planned on staying a week, and I thought while I was here I might look for a job here.

LILY DALE. Where?

HORACE. In Houston.

LILY DALE. Why?

HORACE. Well, I just thought it might be nice to live near you and Mama for a change.

LILY DALE. Oh, you couldn't live here, Brother. There is no room here at all.

HORACE. I didn't mean here. I meant somewhere in Houston, but near you.

LILY DALE. What could you do in Houston, Brother?

HORACE. Maybe I could get a job working in a store.

LILY DALE. Doing what?

HORACE. Waiting on customers like I've always done.

LILY DALE. Have you ever been in a store in Houston?

HORACE. No.

LILY DALE. Well, you'd change your tune if you ever did. They

18

have beautifully dressed men and women working in those stores. Cultured men and women. Not country people.

HORACE. Well, then I thought Mr. Davenport might help me find work at the railroad.

LILY DALE. Doing what?

HORACE. I don't know.

LILY DALE. Do you know, Brother, they are laying off people down at the rail yards all the time? And if Mr. Davenport wasn't such an exceptional worker, he would be in mortal danger of losing his job. Goodness, Brother, be practical.

CORELLA. Albert writes he is opening a dry goods store in Harrison. Maybe he will give you a job. Let's all go to the Palace this afternoon and see a play. I'll fix an early supper for us when we get back. Would you like that, Horace?

HORACE. Sure!

LILY DALE. Have you ever seen a play?

HORACE. Sure. A lot of times at the Opera House in Harrison. I heard Chauncey Olcott sing there, too, last Spring. When he sang "Hello Central, Give Me Heaven," there wasn't a dry eye in the house. And then he sang "My Wild Irish Rose" and the audience went wild! They just tore the house down.

CORELLA. I'll get dressed. *(She picks up the laundry basket and starts out but stops.)* I don't know how to tell you this, Son, but you won't be able to stay a week after all. You see Mr. Davenport...

LILY DALE. *(Interrupting.)* I told him about Mr. Davenport. An' I told him he didn't want you to have him in the first place. Are you gonna give Brother money for a ticket home?

CORELLA. Yes, I am.

LILY DALE. Where are you getting all this money from, Mama? Buying tickets to plays and train tickets for Brother?

CORELLA. It's none of your business, Lily Dale. I have a little of my own, you know, from the sewing I take in now and then. What I'm trying to say, Son, is that I think we can only have you stay just today and tomorrow, at this time.

HORACE. Yes, Ma'am.

19

CORELLA. I'm awfully sorry.

HORACE. Don't worry about it. *(Corella exits U.R. with laundry basket. Lily Dale peeks out door to make sure Corella has gone.)*

LILY DALE. *(Crosses to Horace.)* Do you have a sweetheart, Brother?

HORACE. No.

LILY DALE. I have one. Don't tell Mama I told you that, though. She'd have a fit. He's a lovely boy. *(Leaning in to him.)* Mr. Davenport can't stand him. He won't let him come to the house. He says he is dissolute. I have to slip out to see him. Mr. Davenport found out just before he left that I had slipped out to see him and he was in a fury. He didn't speak to me until the morning he left for Atlanta. He can be very moody, Brother. He is usually very sweet to me, but sometimes he comes home from work and he looks so unhappy. Why do you think our stepdaddy is so unhappy?

HORACE. I don't know, Sister. I've seen very little of him anytime — unhappy or otherwise.

LILY DALE. Mama says it is because of the terrible childhood he had. He doesn't tell us much, but she knows he was supporting his mother and five brothers and sisters when he was twelve. She says all he's ever known is hard work. *(She pulls out a chain that she has hung around her neck. It has a "going steady" ring on it that is hidden under her dress. She shows this to Horace.)* This is the ring my boyfriend gave me. He wants to marry me. He thinks I'm beautiful. He thinks I'm pretty enough to be an actress. He's very handsome, too. He does drink, though. And smokes cigarettes. I told him he would have to stop both before I married him. I told him I had a father who was a drunkard and a cigarette fiend and that those habits had killed him. *(A pause.)* Do you remember Papa?

HORACE. Sure.

LILY DALE. I don't have a picture of him. Do you?

HORACE. No.

LILY DALE. I wonder if anyone has a picture of him? I tell you I can hardly remember anymore what he looked like. Sometimes, I remember him looking one way ... sometimes another. *(A pause.)* Well ... it can't be helped. I can hear his voice, though. I can remember the way he always called me Sister and you Brother.

HORACE. He never called you Sister or me Brother.

LILY DALE. Yes, he did.

HORACE. No, he didn't.

LILY DALE. Yes, he did!

HORACE. No, he didn't! He always called me Horace, Junior and you, Lily Dale.

LILY DALE. Who called me Sister and you Brother?

HORACE. I called you Sister and you called me Brother. But Papa... *(He takes a handkerchief out of his jacket pocket. A pocket watch is wrapped lovingly inside. He shows it to Lily Dale.)*

LILY DALE. What's that?

HORACE. Papa's watch. It doesn't run. I'll have it fixed someday. It has his initials engraved, see...

LILY DALE. Where did you get it?

HORACE. I found it stuffed in a drawer at the house when I came back after you all had gone that time. And look here... *(He takes a wedding ring out of his pocket.)* This is Mama's wedding ring.

LILY DALE. How do you know?

HORACE. Look inside. It says to C.T from H.R.

LILY DALE. Yes, it does.

HORACE. I used to have some of Papa's books.

LILY DALE. Where are they now?

HORACE. I don't know. They just disappeared after I went out to work at the Taylor plantation. I used to read all the time, when Mr. John Howard was alive. I read newspapers now, mostly.

LILY DALE. I can't stand reading. Mama doesn't like to read either.

HORACE. I know.

LILY DALE. Mr. Davenport says he's never read a book in his life and doesn't intend to. When Mama told him once how Papa used to like to read, he said, "No wonder he drank." *(She takes another peek out U.R. door, then runs to the piano bench, lifts up the seat cover and takes out a picture. She crosses back to Horace.)* This is my sweetheart. Isn't he good-looking? He plays baseball on the city team. He's first baseman. He's a wonderful athlete. He's twenty-two. Mr. Davenport says he's old enough to be my father, but I think a boy should be quite a bit older than a girl. Don't you?

HORACE. I hadn't thought about it one way or the other. *(Corella enters U.R. dressed for the theatre. She has her gloves on and carries a purse and hat. As she enters, Lily Dale jumps up and goes to the slipper chair D.S. of the piano where she hides the picture of Will under the seat cover. She takes her gloves from the back of the chair.)*

CORELLA. Are you ready? *(She crosses up into the hallway by the coat rack and looks into the mirror as she puts on her hat.)*

LILY DALE. What are we going to see?

CORELLA. I don't know, but I'm sure it will be good. It usually is.

LILY DALE. I like music best. We went to hear Galli-Curci when she sang here and Paderewski and John McCormack.

HORACE. I would like to have heard him. I love Irish tenors. I heard Chauncey Olcott.

LILY DALE. I know. You told us.

HORACE. Did John McCormack sing "Mother Macree"?

CORELLA. Yes, he did.

HORACE. So did Chauncey Olcott. As an encore.

CORELLA. We have a record of John McCormack singing. Play it for him, Sister. We have time. *(Lily Dale crosses R. to the Victrola and puts the record on. We hear John McCormack singing "Child's Song."* Once the music starts Lily Dale slowly turns and looks at Horace as the lights fade.)*

Scene 3

A few hours later. About five o'clock. There is a beautiful late afternoon sunlight coming in through the window. The room is empty for a moment. Then Corella comes in followed by Lily Dale and Horace. Lily Dale is carrying a program from the

*See Special Note on copyright page.

22

theatre. She crosses to the piano and sets it down. She sits on the piano bench. Corella sits on the couch. Horace sits on the chair by the U. wall.

LILY DALE. I don't believe you cared for the play, Brother.

HORACE. Yes, I did. What I could understand.

CORELLA. He's never seen Shakespeare before, Sister. He can be hard to understand at first.

LILY DALE. *(Laughing.)* You went to sleep twice. Once you were snoring so loud I had to poke you. Mama, what did Papa call me? Did he call me Sister or did he call me Lily Dale?

CORELLA. I don't remember.

LILY DALE. I think he called me Sister, but Brother says he called me Lily Dale.

CORELLA. Yes, he did call you Lily Dale. I remember now.

LILY DALE. All the time?

CORELLA. I think so; he thought we should all be called by our given names.

LILY DALE. How old were you when you married our father?

CORELLA. Eighteen. I had Horace when I was nineteen.

LILY DALE. How old was our father?

CORELLA. Twenty-two. We were all moving around everyplace after the war. We had lived for awhile in Goliad and then gone to Salurie Island where my papa was in charge of a lighthouse; but then there was a terrible storm and the water came up to the second story of our house and Papa couldn't get to us, and we almost drowned. Anyway, when the storm was over my papa took us off the island and we went back to Goliad and then we moved back to Harrison, because he was trying to save some of the land from his papa's plantation he'd been cheated out of. And I think your father was already there then. I believe they had moved there by that time from Galveston. He was very handsome, I remember. Very distinguished, even as a young man. *(Pete Davenport has entered quietly through his bedroom door off the hallway U. He hears the end of this.)* His brothers had started a newspaper. He had a law office. *(Pete*

23

slams the bedroom door and enters the room. Both Lily Dale and Corella scream in surprise and fright. Lily Dale runs to the couch and lands on the D. end of it. Horace jumps up out of his chair and backs into the hallway so Pete can't see him.)

PETE. *(Chuckling.)* Don't be frightened.

CORELLA. Oh, you gave me such a start.

LILY DALE. Oh, me too. I couldn't imagine who you were or what you wanted.

CORELLA. Oh ... *(She laughs with relief.)* I don't know when I've been so frightened. My heart is beating so. I didn't know who it was. When did you get here?

PETE. I've been here two hours. I took a nap. *(He sits in the Morris chair, U.R.)*

LILY DALE. We got your letter. But we didn't expect you until tomorrow. *(She takes a throw pillow from the couch and puts it behind Pete's head. She hugs and kisses him.)* I am so glad you're home. I have missed you so much. I learned two new pieces while you were gone. I just love my new piano. *(Pete turns on the lamp next to his chair. Lily Dale arranges her music, then turns on the lamp on the piano.)*

CORELLA. *(Standing and crossing up to Horace. She brings him into the room a bit.)* Pete. This is my boy. This is Horace. *(A nervous laugh.)* He surprised us this morning by walking in here. He said he decided to take the day off and pay us a visit.

HORACE. Hello, Sir.

PETE. *(Very cold.)* Hello.

CORELLA. *(Nervously.)* Did you have a good time, Mr. Davenport?

PETE. Yes, I guess so. *(He stands and starts to head out of the room.)*

CORELLA. How were your people?

PETE. All right. *(He exits to his room U.R.)*

LILY DALE. Oh, he's mad. He can be the sweetest thing in the world, but when he's crossed, he can be a terror. I only saw him mad once and I hope to never see it again.

CORELLA. *(Leading Horace toward the front door. It's almost a push towards it.)* Horace, there's no room here for you now. You see, Sister was going to sleep with me in my bed and I was going to give you her bed, but now ... You can get a train back to Harrison tonight. You go right to Virgie and explain just what happened and she'll put you up. I know Albert will give you a job in his store.

HORACE. *(Stopping her with his words.)* I don't have any money for my ticket home.

CORELLA. Oh, yes. I forgot. *(She looks in her purse.)* You wait here. I have my money in my sewing closet. I'll be right back. *(She hurries out U.R. with purse, hat and gloves.)*

LILY DALE. How are all our old friends in Harrison?

HORACE. All right. Willie Roseberry left.

LILY DALE. *(To Pete who comes back in.)* Mama has gone to get him money to get back home on. She sent him two dollars to get here and she...

PETE. *(To Corella who comes back in.)* Are you giving him money?

CORELLA. Well ... you see, Mr. Davenport...

PETE. You're a grown man. Aren't you ashamed to take money from your mama? When I was your age, I had been supporting my mother and my brothers and sisters for twelve years. Nobody ever gave me anything and I never asked anyone for anything. What kind of man are you gonna make taking money from a woman at your age? *(He exits to his room U.R.)*

CORELLA. He doesn't mean that. He's not as bad as he sounds. Take the money. *(She gives it to him. They hug. He leaves. She watches him through the front door.)*

LILY DALE. *(At piano, calling.)* Mr. Davenport. He's gone. Come listen to my new pieces. *(She starts to play the Mozart Sonata in C Major.)*

CORELLA. Be quiet, Lily Dale. I have a splitting headache. Just be quiet for once. *(She exits U.R. Lily Dale continues playing, but in a subdued manner.)*

PETE. *(Entering and crossing to his chair. He sits.)* Play the Etude I like.

25

LILY DALE. All right. *(Pete starts to read the newspaper he has carried in with him.)* I won't play if you're going to read the paper.)

PETE. *(Putting the paper down on the table next to his chair.)* I'm not going to read the paper. *(Lily Dale begins to play the Chopin Etude. There is a knock on the door. Pete goes to it and opens it. Horace is there. Lily Dale stops playing.)*

PETE. What do you want?

HORACE. I forgot my suitcase. *(Corella enters and crosses to him by the door.)* I forgot my suitcase.

CORELLA. Oh ... *(She gets it, gives it to him and he puts it down.)*

HORACE. I brought some presents for you all. *(He opens the suitcase and takes out three gifts, all wrapped with brown wrapping paper. Two have ribbon around them. The third, which is Pete's, has string around it. He gives Corella her gift.)*

CORELLA. Thank you, Son. *(She opens it. It is a painted cup and saucer.)* That's certainly pretty. I do appreciate it.

HORACE. *(To Lily Dale who ran over the minute "presents" were mentioned.)* And this is for you, Lily Dale. *(He hands it to her. It is a memory book. He hands Mr. Davenport his package of cigars.)*

LILY DALE. *(Unwrapping her gift on the piano bench.)* I got one of these already. Anyway, I haven't been to school in four years. Mr. Davenport said I could just stay home and practice the piano and compose music.

CORELLA. She wrote a rag. She called it the Davenport Rag for her stepdaddy. What did Horace bring you, Mr. Davenport? *(He holds up unwrapped cigar box.)* That's nice.

PETE. It would be if I smoked. *(He puts them down and continues to read the paper.)*

CORELLA. You can give them to somebody at the train yard.

PETE. I expect I can. *(There is an unkind pause.)*

CORELLA. You tell Virgie and the rest of them, hello, if you see them.

HORACE. I will. *(He starts out.)*

CORELLA. Goodbye again, Son.

26

HORACE. Goodbye.

CORELLA. And don't forget to tell Albert you are looking for a new job.

LILY DALE. Mama, why did you do that?

CORELLA. *(Watching Horace from inside the front door.)* Do what?

LILY DALE. Tell Mr. Davenport about the rag I composed. I wanted to surprise him.

CORELLA. I'm sorry.

LILY DALE. It was to be his Christmas present. I was going to play it for him on Christmas morning. *(She crosses L. to the trunk D. of the couch and opens it. Inside is the music she has written. She takes it out and crumples it up as she goes back to the piano.)*

PETE. You can write me another one for Christmas. You can call that one the Christmas Rag. You play this one for me now.

LILY DALE. All right. *(She opens and smooths out the crumpled music, hands it to Pete. She starts to play the Davenport Rag.* * *Corella goes to the window and looks out.)* What are you looking out the window for? *(Corella doesn't hear her. She stops playing.)* What are you looking out the window for?

CORELLA. What?

LILY DALE. I said why are you looking out the window?

CORELLA. I just wanted to see if your brother got on the street-car all right. You go on playing.

LILY DALE. No. I don't want to play unless everybody is going to listen.

CORELLA. I'm listening, Lily Dale.

LILY DALE. You're not listening if you're looking out the window.

CORELLA. All right. *(She sits on the couch.)* Now I'm listening. Go ahead and play. *(Lily Dale continues with her rag as the lights fade.)*

---

*See Special Note on copyright page.

27

Scene 4

About two hours later. As the lights are brought up, we see Pete asleep in his chair. Corella is darning some socks on the couch. Lily Dale is sitting on the floor by the foot of the couch playing with the "going steady" ring that's around her neck. She is thoughtful.

LILY DALE. Mama?

CORELLA. Yes?

LILY DALE. Can I see Will again?

CORELLA. No. *(She pulls Lily Dale D. by the stove.)*

LILY DALE. Why not, Mama?

CORELLA. You know why not. Mr. Davenport doesn't approve of him.

LILY DALE. I like him, Mama.

CORELLA. You're too young to know whether you like him or not.

LILY DALE. If he promised to stop drinking, could I see him?

CORELLA. No, because he wouldn't do it.

LILY DALE. Yes, he would. I know he would. *(We hear a trio of young men out in the yard. They start to sing "Juanita.")* * That's Will. He's come to serenade me. *(She looks out window.)*

PETE. *(Waking up.)* What's that?

CORELLA. *(Looking out front door window.)* It's Will Kidder. He's come to serenade Lily Dale again.

PETE. I think he's crazy. Doesn't he know there are working people that live here? *(He goes to front door and looks out window.)* Mr. and Mrs. Westheimer go to bed at eight o'clock. They work hard all day long and they are tired. Send him away, Lily Dale. *(He crosses back into the living room and heads for his bedroom.)* I forbid you to have anything to do with him. I've told you and told you that.

*See Special Note on copyright page.

28

LILY DALE. *(Catching him by the arm before he gets out of the room.)* And I've told him, Mr. Davenport, I have. *(Pete runs back to look out front door. Lily Dale follows him.)* I've told him and told him, but he says he will just die if I never see him again. He says he is going to reform and never drink again as long as he lives.

PETE. *(Crossing back into the room a bit. They are now face to face.)* I don't believe it. He'd tell you anything to see you. Tell him to clear out of here or I'm going to. *(Pete crosses towards his room.)* I think he's crazy coming around people's houses this time of night acting that way. *(Lily Dale begins to cry. She runs to the couch and throws herself on the floor by the foot of the couch. She is sobbing with her head on the couch. This stops Pete.)* What's the matter with you, Lily Dale?

LILY DALE. You're just breaking my heart. That's what's the matter with me. You're breaking my heart. I love him and he loves me.

PETE. Come on now. Don't cry. Just don't cry now.

LILY DALE. I can't help it. My heart is breaking. I'm so unhappy and so miserable. *(Pete looks at Corella helplessly.)*

CORELLA. Come on now, Lily Dale. You can't hear the singing if you're gonna cry like this.

PETE. Don't cry, Lily Dale. Please stop crying. You won't have to send him away. Just don't cry!

LILY DALE. Will you talk to him?

PETE. What about?

LILY DALE. About ... about how he's reforming. About how he intends to behave himself from now on.

PETE. All right, I guess so.

LILY DALE. *(Stands up, wipes her eyes. Crosses U. to look in mirror in front hallway. Fixes her hair and opens door.)* Will ... Will, come on inside. Mr. Davenport will speak to you now. *(The singing stops. We hear words of encouragement from Will's buddies. Things like "Go get her, boy" and "Good luck, Will!" Will comes to the door. He is a tall, well-built, young man of twenty-two. He seems very sure of himself. He steps into the room.)*

WILL. Evening, folks.

CORELLA. Good evening, Will.

WILL. I hope you didn't mind the serenade.

CORELLA. It was very pretty. "Juanita" is one of my favorite songs.

WILL. *(Looks at Lily Dale for encouragement. She motions for him to talk to Pete.)* Lily Dale says you object to our seeing each other because of my habits. *(No answer.)* Did Lily Dale tell you I'm changing my habits? I've stopped drinking.

CORELLA. We're glad to hear that, Will. You won't ever regret that, I'll tell you.

WILL. No, Ma'am. I know that. I never drank a whole lot anyway.

PETE. What do you call a whole lot? I saw you drunk three times.

WILL. Those were the only three times in my whole life I was ever drunk. I said to Lily Dale, I said, "Wouldn't you know the only times in my whole life I got drunk, I had to meet your stepdaddy?"

PETE. She's too young for you. She's only eighteen. An eighteen-year-old girl has no business...

LILY DALE. I'm almost nineteen, Mr. Davenport. I'll be nineteen next month.

PETE. Well, if you want to come call on her here, all right. But you'll have to sit right here. She can't leave the house with you until she is nineteen. And if I ever so much as smell one drop of liquor on your breath ... you'll not be allowed back in here ever again.

WILL. Yes, sir.

LILY DALE. Oh, thank you, Mr. Davenport. Thank you.

PETE. Now go on, so we can get to bed around here. *(Lily Dale runs over to Will and takes his hand for a moment. She lets go, he leaves, and she runs back to hug Pete. The singing begins again. We hear "Let Me Call You Sweetheart, I'm In Love With You,"* as they go down the street.)*

LILY DALE. Oh, Mr. Davenport. You are the sweetest man in the whole world. You have made me so happy and you have made Will so happy. *(Pete goes back to sleep in his chair. Corella continues*

---

*See Special Note on copyright page.

30

darning socks. Lily Dale sings along with the trio under her breath. There is a knock on the door. Lily Dale heads towards it.)

CORELLA. Do you think that's Will?

LILY DALE. No, I saw Will walking away, singing with the others.

CORELLA. Don't open the door then. It's awful late. You'd better let Mr. Davenport answer it. *(Another knock.)* Mr. Davenport ... Someone's at the door ... Mr. Davenport...

PETE. *(Calling.)* Who is it?

HORACE. *(From outside.)* It's Horace.

PETE. Who? *(Crossing towards door. Lily Dale follows.)*

HORACE. Horace ... *(Pete goes back to the chair. Lily Dale goes to piano bench.)*

CORELLA. *(Nervously.)* I think it's Horace. *(She goes to the door.)* You say you're Horace?

HORACE. Yes, Ma'am.

CORELLA. *(Opening the door.)* What happened, Horace?

HORACE. I took the wrong streetcar and by the time I got to the railroad station the train had gone. There is no train to Harrison until the morning.

CORELLA. Oh, I'm sorry. Did you hear that, Mr. Davenport?

PETE. Don't you have enough sense to get on the right streetcar?

HORACE. I didn't know there were different streetcars.

CORELLA. Of course you didn't. How were you to know that?

HORACE. I thought all the streetcars took you to the railroad station. But they don't. The one I took ended up in the Heights someplace. *(Pete walks out of the room.)*

LILY DALE. Brother, guess what happened? You know the young man I was telling you about? Will Kidder? Tonight after you left he came around to serenade me with some friends. He thought Mr. Davenport was still in Atlanta, I guess, but he wasn't. *(Horace has begun to tremble.)* What are you trembling about, Brother? Are you sick? You look so pale.

31

CORELLA. Are you all right, Son?

HORACE. I don't feel well, Mama.

CORELLA. You're feverish. Your head is on fire with fever. I think you've got malaria. Have you been taking your quinine and calomel regular?

HORACE. Yes, Ma'am. I don't know what's wrong with me. *(He faints on the floor. Lily Dale screams.)*

CORELLA. *(Calling.)* Mr. Davenport ... Mr. Davenport ... Mr. Davenport... *(Pete comes into the room. He eyes Horace without an ounce of compassion.)* Help me lift him up on the sofa ... Please.

LILY DALE. *(Crying.)* Oh, he's gonna die. I know he's gonna die. That's another one of my terrible dreams. I'm always seeing Brother dead in his coffin. Sometimes he is drowned in the river, sometimes he has been in a terrible train wreck, sometimes...

CORELLA. Sh, Lily Dale, sh... *(She covers Horace with the quilt and gets the pillow from U.)*

PETE. He's not going to die. He's just got a fever, Lily Dale.

CORELLA. Feel his forehead. I think he has a very high fever.

PETE. *(Feels his forehead.)* Yes, he does.

CORELLA. Do you think it's malaria? It's just rife down home.

PETE. I don't know anything about malaria. *(He goes to the lamp on the piano and turns it off.)* I don't come from the swamps and the bottoms, remember? I come from Atlanta. The best climate in the world.

CORELLA. Do you mind if he stays here tonight?

PETE. What else can he do? I hope he doesn't lose his job tramping around the country this way.

LILY DALE. He was about to quit his job. He was hoping to find one here in Houston working in a department store. I told him that was the craziest idea I ever heard of. He could never get a job in a Houston department store. He's not qualified. And then he said maybe you could get him a job in the railroad yards and I said, "Brother, that is even wilder yet. Do you know they're laying off people in the railroad yards and it's only because of the great respect they have for Mr. Davenport's abilities down there that he has a job at all."

CORELLA. Sh, Lily Dale. Now, sh!

PETE. He'd better not ask me for a job. Let him get his own job. Nobody ever helped me get a job. I've never asked anybody for anything. Not one solitary thing. I'd have too much pride to ask help of anyone. *(He exits to his bedroom and slams the door. Corella feels Horace's head, again, as the lights fade to black.)*

CURTAIN

ACT II
Scene 1

Two weeks later. As the lights are brought up we see Horace asleep on the couch. It has been made into a sickbed with a sheet, pillow and the quilt. On the end table U. of the couch is a bowl with a cloth in it. Corella uses this to wipe his forehead. There is also a glass of water. Lily Dale tiptoes in from U.R. and goes to her piano. She very quietly plays a few notes. She turns to look at Horace who has been awakened by this.

LILY DALE. Brother?

HORACE. Yes?

LILY DALE. How do you feel?

HORACE. Better.

LILY DALE. Well, I'm glad. Welcome back to the land of the living.

HORACE. Thank you.

LILY DALE. This is the first time in a week you have responded to us at all. We were so afraid for you, Brother. We thought we were going to lose you.

HORACE. Was I sick?

LILY DALE. Sick? I guess you were sick. At the point of death for almost two weeks.

HORACE. I was?

LILY DALE. Out of your head nearly the whole time ... talking the wildest kind of nonsense.

HORACE. I was?

LILY DALE. I tell you, it was awful. Night before last, Mama, Will and I had to hold you in bed by sheer force. You thought Mr. Davenport had a butcher knife and was trying to kill you. You kept screaming, "He's trying to slit my throat. Don't let him slit my throat." Mrs. Westheimer heard you all the way upstairs and thought we were being murdered and made Mr. Westheimer go

34

for the police.

HORACE. My goodness.

LILY DALE. There was a great deal of excitement then, let me tell you. There's good come from it, though. You know what happened? Will came to call the next night, like Mr. Davenport said he could, and made himself so helpful, Mama and Mr. Davenport fell in love with him and he's been invited over every night for supper.

HORACE. He has?

LILY DALE. Yes. And when Mr. Davenport heard day before yesterday he had lost his job, he took him right down to the railroad yard and got him a job working there. Now they ride the streetcar together every day to and from work, and Mr. Davenport says I can marry Will as soon as he saves a little money. Isn't that thrilling?

HORACE. Where am I?

LILY DALE. What, Brother!

HORACE. Where am I?

LILY DALE. Where are you? Oh, heavens, Brother, don't scare me that way. You're in Houston. Don't you know where you are?

HORACE. How did I get here?

LILY DALE. How did you get here? On the train.

HORACE. How long have I been here?

LILY DALE. Two weeks. You've been sick the whole time. Don't you remember? I had to go over to my girlfriend's to practice my music.

HORACE. Have I been baptized?

LILY DALE. What, Brother?

HORACE. Have I been baptized?

LILY DALE. Oh, Lord, Brother! I don't know.

HORACE. Have you been baptized?

LILY DALE. I don't know that either. What makes you ask a question like that at a time like this?

HORACE. Is Mama here?

LILY DALE. No, she went to the store to get me some material.

She's going to make me a ball gown. Will is taking me to a dance. Mr. Davenport says we can go unchaperoned. Isn't that sweet of him? Would you like a little music to cheer you up? I've just gone crazy over rags. I wrote the "Davenport Rag"* *(She plays part of it.)* for Mr. Davenport, and then I wrote the "Willie Rag"* *(She plays again.)* for Will. And now I'm working on the "Lily Rag"* which I'm dedicating to myself. *(She plays this now. All sound pretty much the same. Corella comes in front door with brown bag. Lily Dale stops playing.)* Well, he's much better. He doesn't remember a thing that's happened to him, but he talks sense now.

CORELLA. You feel better, Son? *(Horace nods that he does.)* Did you give him any nourishment, Lily Dale?

LILY DALE. No.

CORELLA. Would you like a little broth, Son? *(He stares at her.)* I bet you would. I'm going to get some for you. You have to keep up your strength, you know.

HORACE. Have I been baptized, Mama?

CORELLA. No, you haven't, Honey. What makes you ask a thing like that?

HORACE. I met this lady on the train coming down here, and she asked me and I said I didn't know. She said I was in mortal danger if I wasn't baptized. *(A pause.)* I thought for sure I was going to die. I was going to die without being baptized.

CORELLA. Well, you didn't die.

LILY DALE. Was I baptized, Mama?

CORELLA. No. I told you that.

LILY DALE. How come we weren't baptized, Mama?

CORELLA. Because every time I started to baptize you when you were babies, something came up to prevent it. Either you got sick, or I got sick, or your father, and then all our troubles started and I just never got around to it. Did you tell him about Mr. Tom Galbraith's store, Lily Dale?

LILY DALE. No.

CORELLA. A terrible thing happened, Virgie wrote me yesterday, his store burned to the ground. Two weeks ago. It must have been right after you left. They say the fire started around three in the morning and by the time they discovered it, it was almost all destroyed. Virgie says the worst part is that since Mr. Galbraith was in debt, people are implying he did it for the insurance, but she says she just heard he had very little insurance. *(Will and Pete come in. They wear overalls and carry lunch pails.)*

LILY DALE. Well, look who's home.

WILL. How does the young man feel?

CORELLA. I think he's going to live now.

WILL. He's strong as an ox. Did you tell him how I had to wrestle with him to keep him in that bed? He thought Pete, here, was trying to kill him.

CORELLA. How was work?

WILL. Fine. I like it better every day. I think they like me. Don't you, Pete?

PETE. Yes, they do. They told me today. They said you're as good a worker as they've ever seen.

LILY DALE. Mama, show them the material and the pattern for my dress. *(Corella takes them out of the bag and hands them to Will.)*

WILL. That's mighty good looking. I'm going to have the prettiest and best-dressed girl at the ball.

LILY DALE. See it, Mr. Davenport? *(She shows it to him.)* Isn't it pretty?

PETE. It sure is.

WILL. *(To Horace.)* Young man, you'd better get well and come go with us.

HORACE. Thank you.

LILY DALE. Can you dance, Brother?

HORACE. Yes.

CORELLA. Virgie taught him. She's the dancer in the family. She loves music and dancing.

PETE. *(To Horace.)* When are you going back home?

CORELLA. He'll be going back before long. He'll have his strength back now in no time, now the fever has broken.

HORACE. I'm going back tomorrow.

CORELLA. No, Son.

37

HORACE. Oh, I'm going to. But first, I'm going to get dressed and get baptized. I'm going to find me a preacher. *(He tries to get up.)*

CORELLA. Oh, Lord. He's delirious again.

HORACE. I'm dirty and I want to be washed clean.

WILL. *(Going to him.)* Come on, fellow. Take it easy.

HORACE. Don't come near me. You're trying to kill me before I can be baptized. *(He is struggling to get up. Will can hardly manage him.)*

WILL. Help me, Mr. Davenport. I can't hold him by myself. *(Pete goes to help Will. They hold him as he struggles and then subsides.)*

PETE. I just think he's putting on an act to get us to keep him here, so he can get free room and board.

CORELLA. Why would anybody want to do that? He's sick and you know he's sick. You should be ashamed of yourself, Pete! *(Horace is exhausted. He closes his eyes.)*

PETE. Does he know he lost his job in Glen Flora?

CORELLA. He didn't lose his job. He just got laid off temporarily.

PETE. That's a polite way of putting it. *(He exits.)*

HORACE. *(Opening his eyes.)* What about my job?

CORELLA. Sh, sh ... now don't get excited, Honey. Everything will turn out all right. You'll see. We'll talk about all that at another time.

HORACE. What about my job, Mama? Don't I have a job in Glen Flora?

LILY DALE. Brother, there has been a terrible fire in Glen Flora. Mr. Galbraith's store burned down. We told you about it.

HORACE. Oh, my God!

CORELLA. But Mr. Galbraith sent word he is building it again. A lovely brick building this time and you can have your job back then. *(Horace closes his eyes as the lights fade.)*

Scene 2

A few days later. As the lights are brought up we see Horace on the couch reading a newspaper. There are two more on the floor beside the couch. Corella comes in.

CORELLA. Well, I don't need to ask you today how you feel. I know you are feeling better. One look at you tells me that.

HORACE. I am. Thank you. Who brought me the papers?

CORELLA. Will did. I asked him to. I hope you like them.

HORACE. Oh, yes, I do.

CORELLA. He asked what you liked and I said, "Oh, anything from out of town." I remembered someone telling me once how you asked everyone you knew going to Houston to bring you back a paper from some other city. What did he get you?

HORACE. *New Orleans Picayune, St. Louis Star* and the *Galveston News.*

CORELLA. The *Galveston News,* that's not very far away.

HORACE. I know, but I like it. It's my favorite paper.

CORELLA. Is that so? Of course, I can't tell one from another. I never read the papers. It's my eyes I guess. You see, I sew so much that my eyes are tired at the end of the day. *(A pause.)* Do you remember Mrs. Clint Harris?

HORACE. No, Ma'am.

CORELLA. She is kin to the Vaughn's some way. Or Mrs. Vaughn, I guess. Who was a Miss Speed, you know, before she married Henry Vaughn. We were friends before I was married. She came to Harrison to work in the courthouse and she lived in a boarding house around the corner from our house, and we used to have her over a lot and...

HORACE. *(Interrupting.)* What about Mrs. Harris?

CORELLA. Oh, yes, excuse me. I ramble so lately. I'll start on one thing and before I know it, I'm off on ten different other subjects. Well, anyway, Myrtle Harris lives across the street in that big house with the stone lions in front. It cost all kinds of money, they say. She called on me when I first came here, but I never returned that call because I'm always working. Virgie wrote me that she had been in Harrison recently and Virgie met her at a bridge club. She told Virgie that I had hurt her feelings, because I hadn't returned her call. Virgie said I hadn't, she was sure, because I was always working. "What does she do?" Virgie said she asked her. "Takes in sewing." Virgie told her. "Oh, heavens!" Virgie said Myrtle said. "Oh, heavens what?" Virgie asked her. "You know she's as poor as you were when you lived here. She didn't happen to marry a rich husband." Virgie said that shut her up. *(A pause.)* Why do you like the *Galveston News* so much?

HORACE. I don't know. I've always loved Galveston, you know.

CORELLA. No, I didn't know that.

HORACE. Oh, yes. I went down there the last three summers when they ran the overnight excursion from Harrison. I loved it. Papa used to talk about it once in awhile, you know, when he was growing up there as a boy.

CORELLA. He didn't grow up there. He was only two years old when the war was over, and his father was killed and his mother had to start the boarding house over in Tyler, so he couldn't remember much about Galveston except what he heard from his mother and brother and sisters.

HORACE. How did they get from Tyler to Harrison?

CORELLA. I don't know. I never heard. I remember your father once talking about his mother and saying that she had never even buttoned or tied her own shoes before the war. She had never lifted her hand to do a single thing. But after it, when they lost their shipping fleet, she had to learn to work and feed a family. And she did.

HORACE. Mama, Will Kidder tells me that for fifty dollars you can go to a business school here in Houston and get a business course. I think I'm going to do it.

CORELLA. Where will you stay?

HORACE. Well...

CORELLA. I'd like to ask you to stay here with us, Horace, but I

40

can't. You understand that. We've no room. We made do while you were sick...

HORACE. No. I know. I didn't expect to stay here.

CORELLA. Where would you stay?

HORACE. Will says I can find a boarding house that's cheap.

CORELLA. How cheap?

HORACE. He didn't say. He just said cheap.

CORELLA. Where will you get the money to do all this, Horace?

HORACE. I'm going to try to borrow it.

CORELLA. I can't help you, Son, you understand that?

HORACE. I wasn't going to ask you, Mama.

CORELLA. Where will you get it?

HORACE. I'll ask Aunt Virgie. Uncle Doc's practice is pretty good now, or I'll try the bank. They might loan me the money.

CORELLA. What if you can't borrow the money?

HORACE. Then I can't go.

CORELLA. Why do you want to study, Son?

HORACE. I don't know. I just don't want to clerk in a dry goods store all my life. There's no future in that, unless you own the store ... which I don't see how in this world I can ever do. I thought if I had a business course, I would have a few more opportunities to get work.

CORELLA. I see. *(A pause.)* I could do this much. I could see that you get a good breakfast every morning. Mr. Davenport leaves for work by five or five-thirty and if you come over here between six and six-thirty, I could fix you a good hot breakfast. I would ask you here to have all your meals, but Mr. Davenport is tired when he comes home and he likes it quiet, and I just don't like to impose on him too much, you know. He's peculiar in many ways, I know, but he has been good to me and your sister. He's no bad habits. Doesn't even smoke, as you know. He worships your sister and he's crazy about Will now. I'm thankful for that, although I tell him not to encourage them too much. Will, you know, wants her to marry him. And, oh, I worry so about it. She seems so young to me to be marrying. Of course, she throws up to me that I was married by this time,

41

too, and I know I was. I wasn't ready for the responsibility of it all. And neither was your father, for that matter. And we had you children so soon. *(A pause.)* Do you have a girl, son?

HORACE. I go with several.

CORELLA. No particular one?

HORACE. I've been seeing quite a bit of Dolly Parker when I come in from Glen Flora. You know she lives with the Garretts now and her two brothers live there too. So there are four young people living there and Mr. and Mrs. Garrett are grand hosts. They have a piano, there are always a lot of young people over there, and Rosa Garrett has a lovely voice. And someone is always there that can play the piano and Rosa has the sheet music of every song you've ever heard of.

CORELLA. Is Dolly pretty, Son?

HORACE. Yes, Ma'am. She is pretty.

CORELLA. And Rosa?

HORACE. She has a very nice disposition and so she has a lot of friends and, like I say, her mother and father are always very kind and hospitable to young people.

CORELLA. Are they still poor as church mice?

HORACE. Yes, Ma'am. I guess they are, but they always seem to have a lot to eat. There is always a ham or a chicken or a turkey on the table, and sometimes they ask as many as twelve or fourteen of us to stay for dinner. Where's Sister?

CORELLA. She's getting dressed for the dance in her room.

HORACE. Where's Mr. Davenport?

CORELLA. He's out in the back yard fixing the chickens' fence so they can't get into his garden. He has quite a garden this year. *(A pause.)* I suppose you'll be thinking about getting married one day.

HORACE. I suppose so.

CORELLA. Have you thought about it?

HORACE. Oh, I've thought about it, but I can't think of marrying now, Mama. I don't even have a job. I want to have a job and at least a few hundred dollars saved before I even think about marrying.

42

CORELLA. And I think that's very sensible. I wish I had been as sensible as that before I married. I hope your sister will be.

LILY DALE. *(Entering U.R. She has on her evening dress and evening slippers.)* How do I look?

CORELLA. Beautiful. Like a picture.

LILY DALE. How do I look, Brother?

HORACE. Very pretty, Sister.

LILY DALE. Thank you. I feel pretty. I thought there just now as I looked at my dress in the mirror, not a girl at that ball, I don't care how rich they are, will have a dress as pretty as mine. Thanks to my sweet mama who sews so beautifully. And works so hard that I can have all these pretty things. *(She kisses Corella.)*

CORELLA. Thank you.

LILY DALE. Where is Mr. Davenport? I want him to see me.

CORELLA. He's out in the backyard working. I'll call him. *(She exits U.R.)*

HORACE. I was thinking, lying on the couch here this afternoon, Lily Dale, Papa used to sing a song to the two of us called "Lily Dale." Do you remember how it went?

LILY DALE. No, and I don't want to. Brother, you always want to talk about the past. I have no interest in it really at all.

HORACE. No?

LILY DALE. No! I want to think of now. This minute. Why do you always want to talk about the past? What Papa did or didn't do? I don't care what he sang and I don't care what he called me. All I know is that he smoked cigarettes like a fiend and was a drunkard and broke my mother's heart, and he died and left her penniless to go out into the world to work and support two children.

HORACE. She didn't support me.

LILY DALE. Well, she supported me. And she's the only one I want to talk about except for Mr. Davenport, who has been more to me than a real father ever could have been. *(Horace pulls the quilt over his head and turns away from her.)* What's the matter with you? Why have you turned your face away? You are jealous of me. That's why. And you should be ashamed of yourself for allowing yourself

43

to be jealous. Mama said that's the Robedaux disposition: jealousy, spitefulness and vindictiveness. I don't have an ounce of it, thank God, and if I thought I did, I'd jump off the highest building in Houston and kill myself. Because that kind of disposition makes you miserable, Mama said. And she doesn't have to tell me that. I see it every time I meet Minnie Robedaux, who teaches school here now in Houston. No matter where she sees me or who I'm with, she stops me and begins a perfect tirade about what she says is her family's side of the story. "I don't want to hear your family's side of anything," I say. "They're your family, too," she says. "Not mine," I told her, "My mother and Mr. Davenport are my family and I want none other. My mother is a living, unselfish angel and I won't have you say a word against her. You and your family mooched off her and my father and drove him to drink. So don't come around here anymore and ask me anything about my father. I only know one thing about him: he died and left us all alone in this world." *(A pause.)* Of course, I hope you're happy now. I was feeling so happy and joyful and you had to spoil all my wonderful feelings, by asking me questions of things I don't want ever again to think about. That's why I love Will. He only talks about the future. What he's going to do with his life, how much he's going to accomplish. He doesn't sit around and talk and wonder why this happened or that happened, or what happened when we were five years old or seven years old. I have not heard him mention his mother or father or childhood once, and he had just as difficult a time as we had. *(A pause. Lily Dale sings, half to herself, "Let Me Call You Sweetheart, I'm In Love With You."* She peeks out the front door curtain, looking for Will.)* Are you going to lie on that couch forever, Brother? You'll never get your strength back lying around on that couch, Mr. Davenport says, and I agree with him. Never. You should make yourself get dressed now every day and start walking around the block at least. *(A pause.)* Why are you so sad, Brother? Why are you always so sad? It's not fair. Turn around and look at me! I can't help it if I have a happy disposition and you don't. Mama said you were never happy even as a child, and I was born with a sweet, loving, happy disposition. Oh, Brother! Brother ... let's be close. I want to be close to my brother, and I feel we aren't. I have to tell you this. We are not close as brother and sister should be. Why, I should be able to come to you with my troubles and I can't. I want to be close, Brother. Please, let's be close.

HORACE. Sister, I feel close to you.

LILY DALE. Do you?

HORACE. Yes.

LILY DALE. And you're not jealous of me?

HORACE. I don't know what you're talking about. I've never been jealous of you in my life.

LILY DALE. Oh, I'm relieved to hear that. I thought you were jealous of me because Mr. Davenport spoils me and prefers me to you. But that's natural, Brother, that he would. You're a stranger to him, really, and I was raised up here in the house with him.

HORACE. I know.

LILY DALE. He's always been so sweet and considerate to me, Brother. You must love him for that. Say you do? Why I remember when Mama decided to marry him and she came to tell me of her decision. And Mama asked Mr. Davenport to come and talk to me after she had told me they would be married. And he came into the living room of the house we rented then and took me in his arms, and he said he was going to be a daddy to me. He was going to see that nothing bad ever happend to me ever again; and that he was going to make up for all the unhappiness I had known in my young life and make up to me for the loss of a father. And he has. He certainly has. And I do love you, dear Brother, but we have lived apart because of circumstances and ... Brother, try to be a little more friendly with Pete. He doesn't mean to be so abrupt. Reach out to him, Brother.

HORACE. I can't stand him.

LILY DALE. Brother, don't say that. I can't bear to hear this.

HORACE. You think I'm faking, lying here on this couch? Do you think if I had the strength right now to walk across this room, I wouldn't do so? Do you think I don't choke on every piece of food of his I eat? How can I get well lying here eating the food of a

45

man I despise?

LILY DALE. Brother! Brother! Brother!

HORACE. I despise him. I despise him. I would never have come here if I had known he would come here and that I would have gotten sick and been at his mercy.

LILY DALE. Stop it! Dear Brother, please ... please!

HORACE. I despise him! I despise him! I despise him! And if I had the srength I would put on my clothes right now and leave. I would leave here right now. *(He falls weakly back on the couch.)*

LILY DALE. Now you've spoiled it for me. I hope you're satisfied, Brother. I do hope you are. You have ruined an evening for me that I had been looking forward to for a very long time!! *(She runs out U.R. crying. Horace tries to get up off the couch. He can't. He tries again, stands, takes a step or two and then falls to the floor. Corella comes in. She sees him on the floor, screams and runs to him.)*

CORELLA. Lily Dale ... Lily Dale ... run for Mr. Davenport in the backyard. Your brother has fallen. He's fainted from weakness. I need help ... Hurry, Lily Dale ... Lily Dale ... can you hear me?

LILY DALE. *(Calling back, weakly.)* I can hear you.

CORELLA. Oh, my God, what's the matter with you?

LILY DALE. Nothing.

CORELLA. You sound so funny. Don't tell me your period has started?

LILY DALE. No, Ma'am.

CORELLA. Then why on earth do you sound so funny?

LILY DALE. No reason. No reason at all.

CORELLA. Then hurry and go for Mr. Davenport. Your brother may be dying for all we know. His father was dead at thirty-two. And bring some smelling salts out of my room. Hurry! Hurry! For God's sake, Hurry! *(She gets one of Horace's newspapers and begins to fan him with it.)* Oh, Son! Son! Please! Wake up! Please!!! *(She is crying. Pete comes in.)* Mr. Davenport ... look here!

PETE. How did he get there?

CORELLA. I don't know. I guess he was trying to go to the bathroom. I went out to call you to see Lily Dale's dress and I

46

stayed and held the lantern for you so you could see to finish nailing the fence, and I came in here to tell Lily Dale you would be here in another five minutes at the most. *(Lily Dale comes running in with the smelling salts.)* And I found him there, half dead, on the floor. Half dead... *(She is sobbing now, Pete takes the smelling salts from Lily Dale and holds it under Horace's nose. Corella controls her sobbing and looks at Horace as Pete administers the smelling salts.)*

HORACE. *(Opens his eyes, sees Pete.)* I despise him. I despise him!

CORELLA. Oh, he's delirious again! Poor boy! He has such a sweet, uncomplaining nature.

HORACE. I despise him! I despise him!

CORELLA. Who are you talking about, boy?

LILY DALE. Pete. Mr. Davenport. *(She is sobbing now.)* He says he hates and despises him.

CORELLA. Sh, Honey... sh ... sh ... he didn't mean that. Never! Never! It's the fever coming back. Don't repeat what he said when he's sick and out of his head.

LILY DALE. He was not out of his head and he has ruined this precious night for me by his hate. *(She runs out of the room, crying. Pete goes after her.)*

CORELLA. *(Cradling Horace in her arms.)* You were out of your mind, weren't you, Son? Tell your sister you were. Don't spoil her evening. Please, Son. She's had so little happiness in her life. So very little. Oh, my God! I want us all so to get along now. *(There is a knock on the door. Corella turns to call to Pete to answer it, but the knock is repeated and she goes herself. Will is there, dressed for the dance with a corsage for Lily Dale.)*

WILL. Hello there, young lady. How do you feel?

CORELLA. Come in, Will. Help me get Horace up on the couch. He fainted.

WILL. *(Going to Horace, picking him up and setting him back on the couch.)* Come on, boy. What did you think you were doing? Up we go.

CORELLA. *(Covering Horace back up.)* Are you feeling better?

HORACE. Yes, Ma'am.

47

CORELLA. You were delirious.

HORACE. Yes, Ma'am.

CORELLA. You kept looking at Mr. Davenport and saying you despised him. Of course, he knew you were delirious and didn't mean a word of it.

WILL. Where's my girl? I thought she'd be all dressed and waiting.

CORELLA. She was, but when her brother fell she got very nervous and upset and ran out of the room. I'll get her. *(She exits U.R.)*

WILL. Did Lily Dale tell you about my new job?

HORACE. No.

WILL. I'm leaving the railroad. I'm going into the produce business. A great new company that's just started up. They have the rights to handle some great new products here in this area. Admiration Coffee; you know, that's the one they advertise as "The Cup of Southern Hospitality." *(A pause.)* Say, you need a job. Speak to Pete about getting my job for you out at the yards. Anyone can do it. *(Horace gives Will a look.)*

PETE. *(Entering U.R.)* Corella says to tell you, Lily Dale will be here in a minute.

WILL. Plenty of time, Pete. Plenty of time. Say, I've just had a great idea. What about Horace for my job in the railroads?

PETE. It's already been taken. It was filled this afternoon.

WILL. That's too bad. We just weren't on the ball, Pete, were we? Why didn't we think about it sooner? *(Pete gives him a look. Lily Dale and Corella enter U.R.)* Say, look here. This sight was worth waiting for. Man ... you are beautiful.

LILY DALE. Thank you, Will! Mama made the dress.

WILL. And it's something! Yes, it is! Doesn't she look gorgeous, Pete?

PETE. Yes, she does.

WILL. Shoot ... she'll be the prettiest girl there, I'll tell you that. What do you think of your sister, Horace? *(Horace looks at her, she looks at him.)* Put a waltz on the Victrola, Pete. Lily Dale and I will show you the Texas Castles: Irene and Vernon. *(Pete goes to put it on.)*

LILY DALE. I don't feel like it, Will. I have a headache.

WILL. A headache!? Well, get over it. No headaches are allowed on this night. We're going to dance all night. *(He takes hold of her and as "The Blue Danube" waltz is heard, they dance a few steps, then stop.)* How is that?

CORELLA. You are both lovely dancers. You make a very handsome couple. What time are you coming home? *(Pete takes the needle off the Victrola and the music stops.)*

WILL. Don't wait up for us.

CORELLA. Oh, I always do. I never close my eyes until she's home.

WILL. Don't you trust me, Lady? Don't you trust me to take care of your daughter?

CORELLA. I trust you, Will. You know that.

WILL. Then you go to sleep.

CORELLA. No. I can't do that. I don't close my eyes until she's in the house.

WILL. What are you going to do when she's married and not living here?

CORELLA. Then, I can't help it. She's somebody else's responsibility.

WILL. What if we're out until dawn?

CORELLA. Then I won't get to sleep until dawn, but surely you're teasing me about dawn. You'll surely be home by twelve.

WILL. Or one.

CORELLA. Twelve!

WILL. All right. Twelve. *(To Lily Dale.)* Let's go, princess.

LILY DALE. All right. Good night, Mama. *(She kisses her.)*

CORELLA. Good night, darling. Have a wonderful time ... both of you.

LILY DALE. Thank you. Good night, Mr. Davenport. *(She hugs him.)*

PETE. Good night, honey.

WILL. Good night, Pete. Don't take any wooden nickels.

49

PETE. I'll try not to. Take care of her now.

WILL. I will.

LILY DALE. Good night, Brother.

HORACE. Good night, Lily Dale.

WILL. Good night, young man, now you take care of yourself. *(They leave. Pete walks them to the door. Watches out the window after them a moment, then steps back C. He stops, looks at Horace who senses this and Horace looks at him. Then away. Pete turns away in disgust and goes to Corella.)*

CORELLA. She did look pretty, didn't she?

PETE. Yes. *(He exits U.R.)*

CORELLA. *(To Horace.)* I told him that whatever you said to him just now, you were delirious.

HORACE. I wasn't delirious, Mama. I knew what I was saying.

CORELLA. Then what possesed you to say it, honey? *(A pause.)* Surely you didn't mean it? *(A pause. Horace doesn't respond.)* I don't think you understand him, is all. He's been good to me and to your sister. He's gruff, I know, and doesn't talk a lot...

HORACE. I'm leaving tomorrow, Mama.

CORELLA. How are you leaving, honey, when you're so weak you can't even make it across the floor?

HORACE. I'm going if I have to crawl out of here. *(A pause.)* I'm going to ask Will to come and help me out of here and ride to Harrison with me on the train ... or put me on the train and I'll make it by myself. And I can make it by myself. Once I get on the train.

CORELLA. I don't want you to do that now. I don't know what's gotten into you and why you are so sensitive, but I tell you...

HORACE. I'm going, Mama. You are wasting your breath. Nothing will keep me here. Nothing!

CORELLA. What will Virgie and the others say, my allowing you to go back that way? Where will you go? You've no job. What will you do?

HORACE. I'll go to Aunt Virgie's. She'll nurse me.

CORELLA. I want to nurse you. I want to do something for you.

50

Please let me. *(A pause. She senses she will never get him to change his mind.)* Anyway, I hope if you come back and study at the business school, I want you to remember what I said to you about having breakfast here every morning. *(Horace closes his eyes.)* You're tired. You want to rest. I'll go now ... *(She starts to exit U.R.)*

HORACE. Mama?

CORELLA. *(She stops.)* Yes, Son?

HORACE. Do you remember that song, "Lily Dale," the one Papa always sang to Sister?

CORELLA. Let's see. I remember his singing it ... but I forget how it goes.

HORACE. Try to remember it, Mama.

CORELLA. Why, honey? *(He doesn't answer.)* Why, honey?

HORACE. Because I want to remember it.

CORELLA. All right. I'll try. I'll certainly try. *(A pause.)* Right now?

HORACE. Yes.

CORELLA. *(A pause.)* I just can't. But I'll keep trying. *(Corella exits U.R. Horace closes his eyes as the lights fade.)*

Scene 3

Later that night. In the background we hear strains of "The Blue Danube" waltz. As the lights are brought up we see Corella waiting for Will and Lily Dale to return. Horace is asleep on the couch. The music has faded out and we can now hear Lily Dale and Will humming the tune outside the front door. Corella hears this and goes to open the door.

WILL. Didn't I tell you I'd get her home by twelve-thirty?

CORELLA. Sh ... sh ... *(She points to Horace. Will and Lily Dale come into the room.)* Did you have a good time?

LILY DALE. Oh, a wonderful time!

51

WILL. We danced every dance. Tell your mother what the reporter from the paper said to you.

LILY DALE. He said I was the most graceful dancer he had ever seen. He thought I should consider dancing professionally.

CORELLA. How was the orchestra?

WILL. Perfection! Show her your present. *(Lily Dale holds her hand up for her mother to see.)*

CORELLA. My goodness!

WILL. How do you like that?

CORELLA. It's beautiful, Will.

WILL. What do you think it cost me?

CORELLA. Oh, I have no idea.

WILL. Plenty. But I thought nothing is too much for my sweetheart.

CORELLA. What does it mean, Will?

WILL. It means we're engaged. I've asked her to marry me.

CORELLA. *(Crying.)* You're too young to be married, darling. Will, believe me. She's too young. I have nothing, absolutely nothing against you, nothing in this world.

WILL. What's the matter with you? We're not getting married tomorrow. I have some sense, you know. I am making my plans. I'm going to work hard for a year and save my money and when I have a few thousand in the bank, we'll marry. Do you have any objections to that plan?

CORELLA. No, I guess not. But promise me you'll wait at least a year. Will you both promise me that?

WILL. I'm not making any promises. I might want to get married tomorrow.

CORELLA. Now, Will, be serious.

WILL. I'm serious. We'll wait as long as you want us to. Won't we, honey? *(Lily Dale nods her head, begins to cry, and runs out U.R.)*

CORELLA. Lily Dale...

WILL. She'll be all right. She's been a little upset all evening. *(He points to Horace, then whispers.)* I think his being here gets her upset. He talked mean to her tonight, she said.

CORELLA. I don't know what all went on. He's upset, too. He says he wants you to take him to the station tomorrow. That he's going home. I don't think he's strong enough to make it by himself, but he says he's determined to go.

WILL. Well, we all have troubles. My brother is about to drive me crazy. He can't keep a job.

CORELLA. Is he older or younger than you?

WILL. Younger.

CORELLA. Your father is dead, isn't he?

WILL. Yes.

CORELLA. Lily Dale says you've been the head of your family for a long time.

WILL. Since my father died.

CORELLA. How old were you then?

WILL. Going on thirteen. I can tell you about hard work. It was up to me to put the food on the table ... if there was any food.

LILY DALE. *(Entering.)* I'm sorry, Will. I bet you think I'm crazy.

WILL. No, I don't. I just think you're sweet and pretty. *(A pause. To Corella.)* Can I kiss her good night? We're engaged.

CORELLA. All right.

WILL. *(He kisses Lily Dale.)* Good night.

LILY DALE. *(In a bit of a daze.)* Good night, Will. *(She slowly sinks on to the piano bench.)*

WILL. *(Heading out the front door.)* Good night, Miss Corella.

CORELLA. Good night, Will. *(Will exits.)*

CORELLA. Well, he's a fine boy. I'm very pleased for you. We better get to bed. *(She starts out U.R.)*

LILY DALE. Mama? ... *(She pauses.)* What do they do to you when you're married to make you have children?

CORELLA. Don't ask me questions like that this time of the night, Lily Dale. Heavens!

LILY DALE. Tootsie says your husband does terrible things to you. Does he?

CORELLA. No. It's not so terrible.

LILY DALE. What is it?

CORELLA. It's just what you have to do with your husband when you get married. That's all.

LILY DALE. What?

CORELLA. You'll find out.

LILY DALE. When?

CORELLA. When you get married.

LILY DALE. Does it hurt?

CORELLA. I've heard some say it does. It didn't hurt me.

LILY DALE. Does it hurt to have children?

CORELLA. Yes, and I pray to God you never have to go through that.

LILY DALE. Will wants children.

CORELLA. He's a fool and don't you ever let him talk you into it.

LILY DALE. Women die in childbirth, don't they?

CORELLA. All the time. Every minute of the hour. While I was having you and your brother, I prayed I would die.

LILY DALE. Why?

CORELLA. Because it hurt so much.

LILY DALE. Which one hurt the most? Me or Brother?

CORELLA. I don't know. I was in terror the whole time I had you both.

HORACE. *(Waking up.)* Is the dance over?

CORELLA. Oh, we've awakened you. I'm sorry. Go on back to sleep.

HORACE. How was the dance, Lily Dale?

LILY DALE. Very nice.

CORELLA. Lily Dale is engaged to be married. Show him your ring.

LILY DALE. *(Crosses to him, shows him her finger.)* It cost a hundred twenty-five dollars.

HORACE. How do you know?

LILY DALE. Will told me. He paid cash for it.

HORACE. You know Papa did sing "Lily Dale" to you when you were a girl, and you got your name from that song. Mama told me.

LILY DALE. *(Pulls her hand away from Horace.)* I don't care whether you're right or not. It doesn't mean a thing to me one way or the other.

HORACE. And Mama ... I remember how the song goes. *(He sings.)*

> Twas a calm still night*
> And the moon's pale light
> Shone soft o'er hill and vale.
> When friends mute with grief
> Stood around the death bed
> Of my poor lost Lily Dale.

CORELLA. *(Having joined in with him on the last line.)* Oh, yes, that's it.

HORACE. You'll have to learn it and teach it to your children, Lily Dale.

LILY DALE. I'm not going to have children.

HORACE. You're not?

LILY DALE. No.

HORACE. Why?

LILY DALE. Because it hurts too much to have children. Mama says she prayed to die while she was having us. Anyway, if I had children I wouldn't sing them that song.

HORACE. Why?

LILY DALE. Because I want to forget everything that happened back then. Everything. I want my children to know about happy times, pleasant things. I don't want to tell them about drunkards and dying and not having enough to eat. And I want you to quit talking to me about it. Every time I feel the least bit good, you begin on all that. What did Papa call us? What did Papa sing? Did Papa do this? Did Papa do that? I don't care about him. How many times do I have to tell you that? I don't care if I ever hear his name again. Mr. Davenport is my father. I want no other. You have no father, but that's not my fault. I have one. The only one I want. *(She runs out U.R.)*

CORELLA. She didn't mean that, you know. She's excited

*See Special Note on copyright page.

55

because, well, you know, the dance and getting engaged and...

HORACE. I don't care, Mama, if that's how she feels.

CORELLA. It might be better if you didn't talk about your papa so much, Horace. You know Mr. Davenport is very sensitive and I don't think he likes it.

HORACE. I don't talk to him about my father. I wouldn't, thank you.

LILY DALE. *(Coming back in. She is still in a fury.)* I'm going to tell you something else! Mama didn't love our papa. She loves Mr. Davenport because he doesn't drink and neglect her; he's been good to her and to me. So don't you ever let me hear you say a word against him again. Because if you do, I'll tell him exactly what you said, and he'll throw you out and never let you in this house again to upset me and Mama. Never! Never! Never! Never! Never!

HORACE. He's not going to throw me out. *(He starts out of bed.)* He'll never get the chance to throw me out. *(He's out of bed.)* I'm getting my clothes on and I'm getting out of here.

CORELLA. Horace, Horace ... it's two in the morning. You can't leave now.

HORACE. Oh, yes, I can. And I will leave. I can leave if I have to crawl on my hands and my knees. *(He takes a step or two, then falls. Lily Dale sees him falling and tries to catch him. Corella screams. Lily Dale holds Horace in her arms.)*

LILY DALE. Oh, Brother. Brother! I'm sorry! Oh, dear Brother! I'm so sorry! I didn't mean a word of those terrible things I said. Not a one. I don't know what gets into me. I have a terrible disposition, Brother, a terrible disposition. It's the Robedaux coming out in me. Forgive me, please, please forgive me. *(She and Horace are crying.)* I loved Papa. Believe me, I did. Just as much as you did. I loved him, but it hurts me so to talk about him, Brother. And it scares me, too. You don't know how it scares me. I wake sometimes in the night, and I think I can hear Papa coughing and struggling to breathe like he used to ... and I didn't mean that about you leaving, Brother. I'm glad you're here and I want you to stay until you're all well and strong again. Because you're the only brother I have and sometimes at night, I see you dead and in your coffin and I cry in my dreams like my heart will break. I am really crying because my crying wakes me up and I say to myself, "Brother is alive and not dead at all, that's just a dream," but still I feel so miserable, I just lie there sobbing, like my heart will break. And sometimes Mama hears me and comes in and says, "Why are you crying, Lily Dale?" And I say, "Because I dreamt again that Brother was dead and had gone to heaven and left us." *(She holds him tighter.)* You're all the family I have, Brother, you and Mama. And we must never leave each other. Promise me you'll never leave me and promise me you'll forgive me. Promise me, promise me...

CORELLA. I know he does forgive you, Lily Dale. He's just too weak to talk much now. *(She goes to Horace.)* Do you think we can help you back on the bed? Or should I call Mr. Davenport? *(She and Lily Dale try to lift Horace to his feet. They can't manage.)* I'd better call Mr. Davenport.

HORACE. Don't you call him. I don't want him to help me. I don't want him near me. I don't want him to touch me. I'll get back on the couch by myself. *(He tries to get up. He can't. He tries again and fails. He slowly begins to pull himself towards the couch. As Horace just gets himself up on to it, Pete comes in with his robe on.)*

PETE. What the hell is going on out here!?

CORELLA. It's all right, Mr. Davenport. Horace fell again, but he's all right.

PETE. What time is it?

LILY DALE. It's two or after.

PETE. Let's go to bed. My God, I have to be up at five, you know. I have to work for a living! *(Pete exits U.R. bedroom door. Lily Dale slowly follows him. As she gets to the hallway, she looks at Horace before she turns and exits U.R. to her room.)*

HORACE. I despise him!

CORELLA. Go to sleep. Get your rest.

HORACE. Mama...

CORELLA. Shh!

HORACE. Mama, Mama...

CORELLA. Shh .. *(She sings a lullabye "Go Tell Aunt Rhodie")*
 Go tell Aunt Rhodie,

Go tell Aunt Rhodie,
Go tell Aunt Rhodie
The old grey goose is dead.
(As she sings the last line, the lights fade.)

Scene 4

One week later. The lights are brought up as we hear Lily Dale playing the Mozart Sonata in C Major. Will is seated on Pete's chair. He listens for a moment then slides onto the piano bench with Lily Dale.

LILY DALE. Will, behave yourself. Mama and Brother may come in at any moment, not to mention Mr. Davenport. You know he's very old fashioned. He would be furious if he knew Mama had left us alone in the house unchaperoned. Now you go over there and sit down and behave yourself. *(He doesn't move. Lily Dale stands up.)* Will...
WILL. I'm not leaving your side until you promise to marry me.
LILY DALE. I promised to marry you, a year from now.
WILL. *(Stands and comes towards her. Lily Dale backs up.)* I don't want to wait a year.
LILY DALE. You told Mama you would. That was our agreement when we became engaged. *(A pause.)* Why are you going back on your word? Why are you doing that to me? And stop looking at me that way. You are making me very nervous. Now go sit down in that chair over there *(She points to the slipper chair D. of the piano.)* or I'm leaving here and I'm going to find Brother and Mother and tell them I won't stay here alone with you because you have not behaved like a gentleman.
WILL. *(Takes another step towards her, she stops him by pointing at the chair. Will stops, shrugs, laughs and goes to the chair and sits.)* Is this

58

how a gentleman behaves?

LILY DALE. Yes. Thank you. *(She goes back to the piano and begins to play.)*

WILL. Lily Dale?

LILY DALE. *(Stops playing.)* What?

WILL. Something is wrong with you.

LILY DALE. Nothing is wrong with me. Now be quiet and let me practice. *(She plays again.)*

WILL. Lily Dale?

LILY DALE. What?!!!

WILL. Something is troubling you.

LILY DALE. Oh, I don't know, Will. I'm very nervous. I think it's Brother's being here. He's been so sensitive and touchy. And it's not easy, four of us living on this one floor. Mr. Davenport has been so silent and morose, too, not his usual jolly self, and poor Mama, she's just torn into little pieces trying to make peace between us all.

WILL. It will soon be over. He's leaving tomorrow.

LILY DALE. I must say it will be a relief to have the house back to ourselves. Brother just doesn't fit in. We all try. I do, Mama does, Mr. Davenport and Brother, too, but he just doesn't fit in. Now you fit in. Isn't that funny? You're here five minutes and you cheer everybody up, and Mr. Davenport begins to talk like a normal human being, but once you leave we're silent and gloomy and unhappy. *(A pause.)* I had this dream about Brother again last night. I dreamt he was dead and this time I didn't cry. I said a terrible thing. I said, "It's about time." And Mama said, "We'll bury him in our family plot here in Houston." And I said, "No, we won't. I'll not have him buried with you and Mr. Davenport and me. I want him buried with his father where he belongs." Wasn't that terrible for a sister to have a dream like that about her brother?

WILL. You probably ate something that didn't agree with you for supper.

LILY DALE. No, I didn't. I'm always having terrible dreams. I dreamt once last week that I was a very old woman and I was a famous concert pianist and I had come to Houston to give a concert

59

and before the concert, I looked out through the curtain into the audience and I called out and I said, "Is Will Kidder there?" "No," they said. "He is dead." "What did he die of?" I asked. "A broken heart," they said.

WILL. Shoot ... don't worry about that dream. I'm not ever going to die of a broken heart.

LILY DALE. Will...

WILL. What?

LILY DALE. Look the other way. I want to tell you something.

WILL. Where shall I look?

LILY DALE. Anywhere away from me. *(He does so.)* I don't want to get married.

WILL. *(He looks at her, she turns away.)* Why?

LILY DALE. Don't look at me, please.

WILL. *(Turning away, again.)* Why?

LILY DALE. Because you're going to hurt me if we do.

WILL. How am I going to hurt you?

LILY DALE. You know.

WILL. Oh. *(A pause.)* Why do you think I will hurt you? Who told you I would?

LILY DALE. Sissy Douglas.

WILL. She's a fool.

LILY DALE. I asked Mama about it, too.

WILL. What did she say?

LILY DALE. She didn't want to talk about it. *(A pause.)* She said Papa didn't hurt her, but some women told her they were hurt by their husbands.

WILL. *(He goes to her and touches her gently.)* I'm not going to hurt you.

LILY DALE. How do you know?

WILL. I just do. *(She cries. He holds her.)* Lily, what's the matter?

LILY DALE. I'm scared. I want to marry you, but I'm scared.

WILL. Now I told you...

LILY DALE. I'm scared that I'll have a baby. I know that hurts when you do and I'll die while I'm having the baby. Mama says it's the worst pain in the world. She said she prayed to die the whole time she was having her children.

WILL. Don't you want to have children?

LILY DALE. I do, but I'm scared to, Will. I'm scared of the terrible pain, and I might die and...

WILL. We don't have to have them then.

LILY DALE. You mean you can get married and not have children? *(She pulls away and looks at him.)*

WILL. Yes.

LILY DALE. How?

WILL. There are ways. Pete and your mama are married, have been for ten years now, and they have no children.

LILY DALE. Pete and Mama?! Oh, my God, Will! What are you saying? Are you saying that Pete and Mama...!?

WILL. Honey, they're married.

LILY DALE. But they're too old, Will.

WILL. No, they're not. Your mama is only 38. She could still have a child, if she wanted to.

LILY DALE. My God Almighty, Will!! *(She goes to couch, begins to cry again.)* I wish you wouldn't tell me things like that. God knows what kind of terrible dreams I'll start having now.

WILL. Honey, I only told you so you could understand that married people don't always have to have children if they don't want to. *(He sits with her.)*

LILY DALE. I don't want to, I mean, I want to, but I'm scared to.

WILL. Then we'll never have them.

LILY DALE. Do you promise?

WILL. I promise. Does that make you happy?

LILY DALE. Yes, it does. It certainly does. *(She hugs him.)* You are so sweet. You are the sweetest person in this whole world.

WILL. *(Returning hug.)* You're mighty sweet yourself. *(They hug for a few moments. Lily Dale giggles as Will puts his hand on her leg. She pushes it away. More hugs and giggles.)*

PETE. *(Coming in front door. They don't hear him. He slams the door. Lily Dale screams.)* What's going on here?

LILY DALE. *(Stands.)* Mr. Davenport, I'm nervous enough without your coming in here and scaring me this way. *(She crosses D.R.)*

PETE. I'm sorry little girl, I didn't mean to scare you. *(He crosses in front of Will and looks at him. Will doesn't look at him.)* Where is your mama? *(Pete knocks Will on top of the head with his knuckles. It makes a loud noise.)*

LILY DALE. She's gone for a walk with Brother to help him get his strength back. *(Pete takes one last look at Will and goes to his chair. He sits.)*

WILL. We're going to lose the old boy tomorrow.

LILY DALE. Uncle Albert's coming for him on the seven o'clock train from Harrison and they'll go back together on the three o'clock.

PETE. Will if Albert doesn't get into a gambling game. I think they're a fool to send Albert. Every professional gambler in Houston knows him.

LILY DALE. He has to go back. He has a store now, you know.

PETE. That never stopped Albert. Nothing has ever stopped him from gambling. Not a job, not his wife, not his children. I'm surprised he hasn't gambled his store away long before this.

LILY DALE. He only opened the store two weeks ago.

PETE. I'm surprised he didn't gamble it away the day after it opened. I'll give him six months. It will be gone and he'll be clerking for someone else again. *(Corella and Horace come in the front door.)*

WILL. Did you have a nice walk?

HORACE. Slow. I had to stop and rest every now and again. *(Horace sits in U. chair.)*

CORELLA. Now, you mustn't be discouraged. Naturally you are weak after that long stay in bed. In another week you won't know yourself.

WILL. I hear you have a job.

HORACE. Yes ... clerking for my Uncle in Harrison.

62

CORELLA. He's going to live for the time being with my sister, Virgie. At least until he gets his strength back. She's a wonderful cook and she loves him.

WILL. Does she have any children of her own?

CORELLA. One. A little girl. Her husband said after he saw what she went through having that one, they could drag him around the courthouse square but he'd never put her through that again. *(Lily Dale leans forward from the piano bench and shakes her finger at Will.)* You hungry, Pete?

WILL. Pete's always hungry. I never knew the time he wasn't hungry.

CORELLA. You do pretty well yourself, Will. Are you going to eat with us?

WILL. No. I'm afraid if I eat another meal over here, you'll send me a board bill. *(He gets up and heads for the front door.)*

PETE. *(Lily Dale looks at him imploringly.)* Now, come on. Stay for supper.

WILL. All right, you don't have to twist my arm. I'll stay. On one condition. That Lily Dale will play for us the rag she wrote for you for Christmas time.

LILY DALE. I want to play you my classical piece, Will.

WILL. No. I don't want any classical pieces. I want something lively. I want one of your rags, and I don't want to wait for Christmas time.

LILY DALE. All right. If I play one of my rags, then can I play one of my serious pieces?

WILL. No. Then you can play another rag.

LILY DALE. Will.

WILL. Nothing serious tonight. This is Horace's last night with us and we want him to leave feeling happy.

LILY DALE. Oh, Will. *(She starts to play. Horace begins to cry and runs out the front door. Lily Dale stops.)* What's the matter with him, Mama?

CORELLA. I think it's weakness. He cried twice on our walk, but then it passed and he apologized. I said, "What was there to apologize for?"

HORACE. *(A pause. He comes back in.)* I apologize. Forgive me.

CORELLA. Don't apologize.

LILY DALE. Shall I continue?

HORACE. Would you play "Lily Dale" for me?

LILY DALE. I don't know "Lily Dale." How can I play it for you?

HORACE. I'll sing it for you. Maybe you can play it then.

LILY DALE. All right. I'll try. *(Horace hums the first verse.)*

CORELLA. You have a sweet voice, Son.

HORACE. No, I don't.

CORELLA. Yes, you do. Sing the words to the song, Son.

HORACE. *(Singing as he crosses D.C. towards Lily Dale.)*
>   'Twas a calm still night*
>   And the moon's pale light,
>   Shone soft o'er hill and vale.
>   When friends mute with grief
>   Stood around the death bed
>   Of my poor, lost Lily Dale.
>   Oh, Lily, sweet Lily,
>   Dear Lily Dale.
>   Now the wild rose blossoms
>   O'er her little green grave
>   'Neath the trees in the
>   Flowery vale.

CORELLA. Can you play it now, Sister?

LILY DALE. *(Making an attempt. Then stopping.)* I can't play that.

CORELLA. Sing it again, Horace.

HORACE. No, that's all right. Maybe I can find the sheet music in Houston someplace and Sister can learn it from that.

LILY DALE. Can I play my classical piece now?

CORELLA. Why don't you play something Horace can sing, Lily Dale? He has such a sweet voice. Do you know "Drink To Me Only," Son? Lily Dale plays that.

*See Special Note on copyright page.

HORACE. No.

CORELLA. What do you know?

HORACE. I know "Love's Old Sweet Song."

CORELLA. Oh, that's lovely. Play that, Sister.

LILY DALE. I don't want to, Mama. I want to play my classical piece.

CORELLA. All right then, honey. Play your classical piece.

LILY DALE. Well, I won't play it if you all don't want me to play it, Mama.

CORELLA. I want you to play it, sweetheart. Why do you think I don't want to hear it?

LILY DALE. No. I don't want to play my piece now.

CORELLA. But we want you to, don't we, Pete?

PETE. Yes, we do. I always like to hear her play her classical pieces. Does it have a lot of runs in it?

LILY DALE. Yes, it does.

PETE. I always love it when you have a lot of runs. Play it for us.

LILY DALE. No. Will doesn't want to hear me play it. He wants me to play rags.

WILL. No. I want to hear your classical piece.

LILY DALE. What about you, Brother?

HORACE. Sure, I want to hear it.

LILY DALE. You're sure, now?

HORACE. Yes, I'm sure.

CORELLA. He's leaving tomorrow. It's the last chance he'll get to hear it.

LILY DALE. Well, all right. *(She begins to play the Chopin Etude in C Minor. She plays vigorously but without talent. The lights fade and a recording of the Etude is now heard.)*

Scene 5

The next day. As the sound fades out, we hear Lily Dale begin to *play "Lily Dale."* The lights are brought up and we see Lily Dale and Corella, who is sitting in the chair D. of the piano. We also see, in a low light, Horace and Uncle Albert sitting on the train.*

LILY DALE. I guess Brother and Uncle Albert are halfway to Harrison by now.

CORELLA. I guess so.

LILY DALE. I hope dear Brother will be happier now that he will work for dear Uncle Albert in Harrison and live with Aunt Virgie.

CORELLA. I hope so.

LILY DALE. Brother has never seemed very happy to me in his whole life. Was he ever happy?

CORELLA. I think so. I hope so.

LILY DALE. Maybe you are born with a happy, contented disposition.

CORELLA. Maybe so.

LILY DALE. I'm happy and contented. I wish Brother could be.

CORELLA. I wish so.

LILY DALE. He's determined, that's for sure. He took Will aside before he left last night and asked him to stop by Goggan's and find this sheet music for me to play for him. *(She takes the "Lily Dale" sheet music off the top of the piano.)*

CORELLA. I'm glad you got to play it for him once, at least, before he left.

LILY DALE. Do you think it is a pretty piece?

CORELLA. I think it is very sweet.

LILY DALE. Do you think the girl on the cover looks like me?

CORELLA. Yes. I guess so.

LILY DALE. I'm prettier, though, don't you think so?

CORELLA. Yes, I do. I think you are much prettier.

LILY DALE. Do you think I'm beautiful?

CORELLA. Yes, I do.

LILY DALE. Will says I'm so beautiful I should be in motion pictures. I hope he is sincere when he says it.

CORELLA. I'm sure he is. He always seems very sincere to me. Will is a very sincere, nice person.

LILY DALE. Mama, Will says that you and Mr. Davenport could, if you wanted to ... I mean, that Mr. Davenport and you...

CORELLA. We what?

LILY DALE. Nothing. I forgot what I was going to ask. *(She goes back to playing the piece very softly. The lights and sound of the train are brought up.)*

ALBERT. How do you feel, Horace?

HORACE. I'm all right.

ALBERT. Would you like a sandwich from the Butcher Boy?

HORACE. No, Sir.

ALBERT. An orange?

HORACE. No, Sir. Thank you. I'm not hungry.

ALBERT. I'm going back in the smoking car for a cigar.

HORACE. Yes, Sir.

ALBERT. Do you want to come back with me? I have an extra cigar.

HORACE. No, thank you. I don't feel like smoking.

ALBERT. I have some chewing tobacco on me, too.

HORACE. No, Sir, thank you.

ALBERT. I may be a while; there is a poker game going on back there, the conductor told me, and I think I'll get into it. I feel very lucky today.

HORACE. Yes, Sir.

ALBERT. But I know you won't tell my wife or Virgie about this.

HORACE. No, Sir. *(Albert tucks a cigar in Horace's coat pocket, pats the pocket and exits. Horace closes his eyes and leans back. The lights fade down a bit and the sound fades out.)*

LILY DALE. *(She stops playing.)* Mama, did you love Papa when you married him?

CORELLA. Yes, I did. I thought I did.

LILY DALE. Who did you love most? Papa or Mr. Davenport?

CORELLA. Mr. Davenport is a good man. He's been very good to me. *(A pause.)* He doesn't seem to like your brother. I wish that would change.

LILY DALE. Brother doesn't like him either. Who do you love the most? Brother or me?

CORELLA. I love you both, honey.

LILY DALE. But you love me the most, don't you?

CORELLA. I love you both.

LILY DALE. I think you love me the most.

CORELLA. You're a girl. You have needed me more, perhaps.

LILY DALE. I'm never going to leave you and you are never going to leave me.

CORELLA. When you marry you will have to leave me, sweetheart, and live with your husband.

LILY DALE. Why can't Will move in here with us?

CORELLA. That wouldn't be practical, darling.

LILY DALE. That's what Will says, too. Anyway, we'll get a house next door and if we can't do that, as close as we can. *(She starts to play quietly again as the lights are brought up on the train.)*

MRS. COONS. *(Entering, she comes up to Horace. His eyes are still closed and he is not aware of her. She looks at him a moment before speaking.)* Excuse me. *(Horace opens his eyes.)* Aren't you the young man I met on the way to Houston three weeks ago?

HORACE. Oh, yes, Ma'am.

MRS. COONS. I thought so. Was that Mr. Albert Thornton from Harrison sitting with you?

HORACE. Yes, Ma'am.

MRS. COONS. I thought so.

HORACE. He's my uncle.

MRS. COONS. Of course. You look terrible, son. Have a spell of malaria?

HORACE. I had a spell of something. I've been pretty sick.

MRS. COONS. You still look sick to me. May I sit and visit for awhile?

HORACE. Yes, Ma'am.

MRS. COONS. *(Sitting beside him.)* I don't know why I'm not down myself as much as I have to bear. Mama said yesterday, "Arabella, where do you get your strength from?" "I don't know, Mama." I said. But I do know, it's my faith that gives it to me. My Christian faith. Mr. Coons got sick again, you know.

HORACE. No.

MRS. COONS. Oh, yes. Lost his job, of course. So we have to move again. I've just taken him into Houston to start another Keeley Cure. He swears this is the last time this will happen. "What's to become of us, Mr. Coons?" I said. "I'm not educated, I can't work and you get sick and can't keep a job." *(A pause.)* Of course, you understand what kind of sickness I'm talking about. Whiskey. That's the kind of sickness I'm talking about. He just can't seem to leave it alone. *(A pause.)* How did you find your mama?

HORACE. She's well.

MRS. COONS. And your sister?

HORACE. Just fine.

MRS. COONS. I bet they were glad to see you and sorry to see you go. Did you ask your mother about your baptism?

HORACE. Yes, Ma'am. I wasn't.

MRS. COONS. Mercy! Sick as you look, I wouldn't put it off any longer. It would be terrible if you died without being baptized. How would you explain that to your Maker?

HORACE. Pray for me, Mrs. Coons.

MRS. COONS. What do you want me to pray about? That you live until you're baptized?

HORACE. No, Ma'am. Just pray for me and my sister and my mother...

MRS. COONS. All right, I will. I don't know your sister and your mother but I'll be glad to include them in my prayers.

HORACE. Now, Mrs. Coons. Pray for us now. This very moment.

MRS. COONS. Why certainly, son. *(She takes his hand and closes her eyes.)* Father... I am turning to you here on this train ... this train filled with miserable sinners ... Father, I turn to you and I ask your forgiveness of our sins and your blessings.

HORACE. My mother and my sister and me. Pray for us, Mrs. Coons, pray for us.

MRS. COONS. Give me time, son. I'm getting to all of you ... Father... *(Lily Dale begins to sing "Lily Dale" as she plays it.)* What's your mother's name, son?

HORACE. Corella.

MRS. COONS. And your sister?

HORACE. Lily Dale.

MRS. COONS. Father, I've been asked to remember in my prayers this young man, Horace, and his dear mother, Corella, and his dear sister, Lily Dale. Father of mercy, Father of goodness, Father of forgiveness...

(The lights and sound fade out on the train. Lily Dale continues singing and the lights slowly fade to black.)

CURTAIN

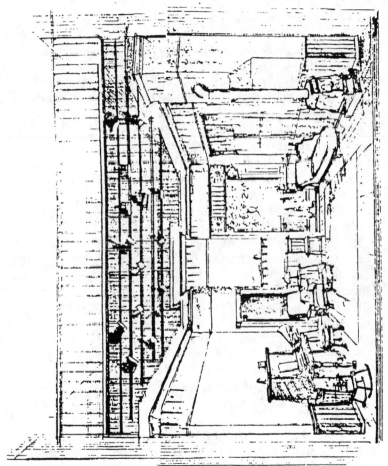

Rendering by Dan Conway of his set for
the New York production of "Lily Dale"

PROPERTY LIST

ACT I

PRE-SET ON STAGE

Sewing box with threaded needles—*U. of couch on floor*

Socks that need darning, needle and darning yarn—*In sewing box*

Patchwork quilt—*Folded on U. end of couch*

Throw pillow—*On top of quilt*

"Davenport Rag" sheet music—*Hidden in trunk D. of couch*

Large coat rack with inlaid mirror—*U. front entrance hallway*

Sheet music—*On half-wall by front door*

Pillow—*Behind half-wall*

Bowl and pitcher—*On coat rack*

Footstool—*D. of Morris chair*

Lily Dale's lace gloves—*On back of slipper chair*

Photo of Will—*Hidden in piano bench*

(2) Records—*On Victrola table, U. end*

(2) Piano books—*On piano*

China doll—*On slipper chair*

Laundry basket full of clean clothes—*U. of Victrola table on floor*

Blue kerchief—*On Pete's table, D. corner*

Blue shirt—no buttons—*Next to sewing box, under couch*

(2) Pairs of pants—*On top of blue shirt*

"Lily Dale" sheet music—*Face down on U. top of piano*

Broom—*U.L. of couch, leaning on wall*

Bucket—*D. of piano*

White skirt—*In wooden bucket*

Blue yarn—*In wooden bucket*

PRE-SET OFF LEFT ON PROP TABLE

Horace's suitcase—appears on luggage rack of train, top of show

(3) Gifts—painted cup and saucer, Memory book and box of
    cigars, all pre-wrapped in brown paper, tied with ribbon or string
    and inside Horace's suitcase
Straw suitcase for Mrs. Coons
(2) Lunch pails
Material and pattern for Lily Dale's dress in brown bag
(3) Letters addressed to Pete and Corella
Corsage in box
Engagement ring
(3) Newspapers
Sheet
Glass of water
Face cloth
Additional pillow
Playbill

PRE-SET OFF RIGHT ON PROP TABLE
Smelling salts
Work gloves
Houston Gazette newspaper
Dishcloth
Bowl of flour
Corella's hat, purse and gloves
Sandwich on plate
Napkin
Glass of milk
(2) Dollars
(3) Pairs of pants for Corella to sew on
Tape measure
Box of pins

ACT II

PRE-SET ON STAGE
Sheet—*On couch*
Extra pillow—*On couch*

(3) newspapers—*In end table U. of couch*
Photo of Will—*Strike from slipper chair*
Pete's slippers—*Floor D.R. of Morris chair*
Leather (Horace's) suitcase—*Strike from hallway*
Straw suitcase—*Strike from train*
Victrola—*Strike record, lift needle*
Sheet music—*Strike from piano*
Broom—*Strike from room*

PRE-SET IN COSTUMES
Pocket watch and wedding ring wrapped in handkerchief—
    HORACE
Cigars, chewing tobacco—ALBERT
"Going Steady" ring on gold chain—LILLY DALE

COSTUME PLOT

ACT I, SCENE 1
MRS. COONS: Dark green skirt, petticoat, brown print blouse, brown belt, hat, gloves, glasses, carpetbag, handkerchief, shoes, hose, shawl and fan

HORACE: Two-piece suit, white shirt, suspenders, socks, shoes, cap, T-shirt, tie

ACT I, SCENE 2
LILY DALE: Blue and white gingham dress, white stockings, shoes, petticoat, gloves (pre-set on stage)

CORELLA: Off-white blouse, petticoat, hose, shoes, lavender skirt, apron. Add: jumper top, gloves, hat and purse (pre-set Off Right)

HORACE: Same

ACT I, SCENE 3
LILY DALE: Same with gloves added

CORELLA: Same with jumper top, hat, purse and gloves added

HORACE: Same

PETE: Three-button "Wallace Beery" shirt, blue trousers, suspenders, socks, shoes

ACT I, SCENE 4
ALL THE SAME

WILL: White shirt, grey trousers, brown jacket, tie, belt, socks, shoes, cap

ACT II, SCENE 1
HORACE: Pajamas, undershirt, boxer shorts, socks

LILY DALE: Same

CORELLA: Dark print blouse, dark rose linen skirt, petticoat, shoes, hose, purse

WILL: Blue and white overalls-distressed and dirty, brownish work shirt, socks, shoes, cap, work gloves (in pocket)

PETE: Brown overalls, white shirt, tie, shoes, socks, work gloves (in pocket), brown fedora

ACT II, SCENE 2
HORACE: Same

CORELLA: Same

LILY DALE: White party dress (no petticoat), white stockings, gloves, shoes

PETE: Work pants, shirt, shoes, socks, belt

WILL: Blue suit, shirt with white collar, bow tie, brown shoes, dark socks, suspenders, handkerchief, flower in lapel

ACT II, SCENE 3
CORELLA: Same

HORACE: Same

LILY DALE: Same

WILL: Same

ACT II, SCENE 1
HORACE: Pajamas, undershirt, boxer shorts, socks

LILY DALE: Same

CORELLA: Dark print blouse, dark rose linen skirt, petticoat, shoes, hose, purse

WILL: Blue and white overalls-distressed and dirty, brownish work shirt, socks, shoes, cap, work gloves (in pocket)

PETE: Brown overalls, white shirt, tie, shoes, socks, work gloves (in pocket), brown fedora

ACT II, SCENE 2
HORACE: Same

CORELLA: Same

LILY DALE: White party dress (no petticoat), white stockings, gloves, shoes

PETE: Work pants, shirt, shoes, socks, belt

WILL: Blue suit, shirt with white collar, bow tie, brown shoes, dark socks, suspenders, handkerchief, flower in lapel

ACT II, SCENE 3
CORELLA: Same

HORACE: Same

LILY DALE: Same

WILL: Same

PETE: Nightshirt, slippers, robe

ACT II, SCENE 4
LILY DALE: Pale green dress, petticoat, shoes, hose

WILL: Blue trousers, white shirt, tie, suspenders, black shoes, socks

PETE: Blue trousers, white shirt, socks, shoes

HORACE: Suit, white shirt, suspenders, socks, shoes, hat

CORELLA: Same

ACT II, SCENE 5
HORACE: Same

CORELLA: Same

LILY DALE: Same

UNCLE ALBERT: Grey, striped suit, tie, vest, black bowler, shoes, socks

MRS. COONS: Dark green skirt, petticoat, black plaid blouse, gloves, carpetbag, glasses

COSTUMES PRE-SET BACKSTAGE
PETE: (1) Brown hat, (1) pair black boots, (1) pair brown overalls, flannel nightshirt and robe, grey pants, flannel shirt (no collar), sweater vest

CORELLA: Lavender jumper top, (1) cameo brooch

77

MUSIC AND SOUND CUES
(Played by Lily Dale as well as recorded on tape.)

CHOPIN ETUDE IN C MINOR (Both)

MOZART SONATA IN C MAJOR (Played by Lily Dale)

LILY DALE by H.S. THOMPSON* (Both)

3 "RAGS" by J. REVELEY* (Both)

CHILD'S SONG by JOHN McCORMACK (Recorded on tape)

STEAM TRAIN RUNNING (Recorded on tape)

WILLIE RAG by J. REVELEY* (Both)

*See Special Note on copyright page.